Understanding Terrorism in America

D0453757

The terrorist attacks on September 11, 2001, seemed to initiate the United States into the full horrors of international terrorism. Yet the country is no stranger to terrorism. Since 1950 there have been over 3,000 terrorist attacks, ranging from the Ku Klux Klan's campaign of terror against the civil rights movement, through the waves of attacks by neo-Nazi and militia groups to the activities of Osama bin Laden's al Qaeda network.

Christopher Hewitt's book is a vivid survey of the causes and strategies of terrorism and governmental responses to it. He examines the organizational structure of terrorist networks, how they are financed, and their ideological agendas. His comprehensive portrait examines the complete spectrum of terrorist groups active in the United States, including Islamic fundamentalists, white supremacists, black militants, revolutionary communists, neo-Nazis, militant Jewish groups, *émigré* groups and anti-abortionists.

This book is essential reading for students of American politics and terrorism. It also provides a highly readable account for interested readers wishing to know the background to a subject which has recently become even more tragically relevant in world affairs.

Christopher Hewitt is Professor of Sociology at the University of Maryland, Baltimore County. He has published widely on all aspects of terrorism and is a regular commentator in newspapers and on television.

Routledge Studies in Extremism and Democracy
Series editors: Roger Eatwell, *University of Bath*, and
Cas Mudde, *University of Antwerp-UFSIA*

This new series encompasses academic studies within the broad fields of 'extremism' and 'democracy'. These topics have traditionally been considered largely in isolation by academics. A key focus of the series, therefore, is the relation *between* extremism and democracy. Works will seek to answer questions such as the extent to which 'extremist' groups pose a threat to democratic parties, or how democracies can respond to extremism without undermining their democratic ideals.

The books encompass two strands:

Routledge Studies in Extremism and Democracy includes books with a broad and introductory focus which are aimed at students and teachers, available in hardback and paperback. Titles include:

Understanding Terrorism in America
From the Klan to al Qaeda
Christopher Hewitt

Routledge Research in Extremism and Democracy offers a forum for new research intended for a more specialist readership, in hardback only. Titles include:

1   **Uncivil Society?**
    Contentious politics in post-communist Europe
    Edited by Petr Kopecky and Cas Mudde

2   **Political Parties and Terrorist Groups**
    Leonard Weinberg and Ami Pedahzur

3   **Western Democracies and the New Extreme Right Challenge**
    Edited by Roger Eatwell and Cas Mudde

Understanding Terrorism in America
From the Klan to al Qaeda

Christopher Hewitt

London and New York

First published 2003
by Routledge
11 New Fetter Lane, London EC4P 4EE

Simultaneously published in the USA and Canada
by Routledge
29 West 35th Street, New York, NY 10001

Reprinted 2003

Routledge is an imprint of the Taylor & Francis Group

© 2003 Christopher Hewitt

Typeset in Times by BC Typesetting, Bristol
Printed and bound in Great Britain by
TJ International Ltd, Padstow, Cornwall

British Library Cataloguing in Publication Data
A catalogue record for this book is available from the British Library

Library of Congress Cataloging in Publication Data
Hewitt, Christopher.
    Understanding terrorism in America: from the Klan to al Qaueda/
    Christopher Hewitt.
        p. cm. – (Routledge studies in extremism and democracy)
    Includes bibliographical references and index.
    1. Terrorism–United States. 2. Terrorists–United States.
3. Radicalism–United States. I. Title. II. Series.
    HV6432.H48 2002
    303.6′25 0973–dc21   2002069858

ISBN 0–415–27765–5 (hbk)
ISBN 0–415–27766–3 (pbk)

Contents

Tables

Illustrations

Series editors' preface

For much of the "short twentieth century," history was characterized by the clash of great ideologies, internal violence and major wars. Although most catastrophic events took place outside the Western world, Europe and the United States were not immune from the turmoil. Two world wars and a series of lesser conflicts led to countless horrors and losses. Moreover, for long periods liberal democracy – especially in its West European form – seemed in danger of eclipse by a series of radical forces, most notably communist and fascist.

Yet by the turn of the 1990s, liberal democracy appeared destined to become the universal governmental norm. Dictatorial Soviet communism had collapsed, to be replaced in most successor states by multiparty electoral politics. Chinese communism remained autocratic, but in the economic sphere it was moving rapidly towards greater freedoms and marketization. The main manifestations of fascism had gone down to catastrophic defeat in war. Neo-fascist parties were damned by omnipresent images of brutality and genocide, and exerted little appeal outside a fringe of ageing nostalgics and alienated youths.

In the Western world, political violence had disappeared, or was of minimal importance in terms of system stability. Where it lingered on as a regularly murderous phenomenon, for instance in Northern Ireland or Spain, it seemed a hangover from the past – a final flicker of the embers of old nationalist passions. It was easy to conclude that such tribal atavism was doomed in an increasingly interconnected "capitalist" world, characterized by growing forms of multi-level governance that were transcending the antagonism and parochialism of old borders.

However, as we move into the new millennium there are growing signs that extremism, even in the West, is far from dead – that we celebrated prematurely the universal victory of democracy. Perhaps the turn of the twenty-first century was an interregnum, rather than a turning point? In Western Europe there has been a rise of extreme right and populist parties, which pose a radical challenge to existing elites – even to the liberal political system. In the United States, the 1995 Oklahoma mass-bombing has not been followed by another major extreme right attack, but there is simmering resentment towards the allegedly over-powerful state among well-armed militias and other groups. More generally across the West, new forms of green politics, often linked by a growing hostility to globalization–Americanization, are taking on more violent forms (the issue of animal rights is also growing in importance in this context).

In the former Soviet space, there are clear signs of the revival of "communist" parties (which often masquerade as "socialists" or "social democrats"), whose allegiance to democracy is (in varying degrees) debatable. In Latin America, there remain notable extremist movements on the left, though not all tend to be communist. This trend may well grow both in response to globalization–Americanization and to the (partly linked) crises of many of these countries, such as Argentina. This in turn increases the threat to democracy from the extreme right, ranging in form from paramilitary groups to agro-military conspiracies.

The rise of Islamic fundamentalism has been an even more notable feature of recent years. This is not simply a facet of Middle Eastern politics. It has had an impact within some former Soviet republics, where the old nomenclature have used the Islamic threat to maintain autocratic rule. In countries such as Indonesia and India, Muslims and other ethnic groups have literally cut each other to pieces.

It is also important to note that growing Islamic fundamentalism has had an impact within some Western countries. The terrorist attacks on the World Trade Center and elsewhere in the United States on September 11, 2001 are perhaps the most graphic illustration of this impact. But in democracies generally, the rise of religious and other forms of extremism pose vital questions about the limits of freedom, multiculturalism, and tolerance. This is especially the case in ones which have experienced notable Islamic immigration and/or which face the greatest threat of further terrorist attack.

Democracy may have become a near-universal shibboleth, but its exact connotations are being increasingly challenged and debated. As long as the "evil empire" of communism existed, Western democracy could, in an important sense, define itself by the "Other" – by what it was not. It did not have overt dictatorial rule, censorship, the gulags, and so on. But with the collapse of its great external foe, the spotlight has turned inwards (although Islam is in some ways replacing communism as the "Other"). Is (liberal-Western) democracy truly democratic? Can it defend itself against terrorism and new threats without undermining the very nature of democracy?

These general opening comments provide the rationale for the *Routledge Studies in Extremism and Democracy*. In particular, there are three issues which we seek to probe in this series:

- Conceptions of democracy and extremism
- Forms of the new extremism in both the West and the wider world
- How democracies are responding to the new extremism.

Christopher Hewitt's book, which launches the *Routledge Studies in Extremism and Democracy*, touches on all three of these key issues, including the definition of terrorism, the nature of the terrorist threat within the United States, and how the US government and other agencies have responded to such threats. Unlike most other books that have appeared since September 11, this is not a quick attempt to profit from the increased interest in terrorism in general, and in the United States in particular. Hewitt's book is the result of many decades of research by one of the leading American scholars of terrorism. Moreover, it draws upon an extensive and unique data set of terrorism in the United States, providing a broad historical study of the phenomenon that goes way beyond the attacks of September 11.

Hewitt has written a book that will shatter many misconceptions. It begins by noting the dramatic impact on American opinion of the September 2001 attacks by al Qaeda terrorists. Many commentators have portrayed these events in terms of a national psychodrama, which tore away the veil of illusions of American impregnability. However, as Hewitt points out in his second chapter, mass terrorism on American soil is not a new phenomenon. Islamic terrorists had previously sought to blow up the World Trade Center in 1993, while in 1995 a right-wing extremist "loner" had bombed a government building in Oklahoma City killing well over a hundred people. Moreover, in the half century before September 11, over 3,000 terrorist offences and more than 700 terrorism-related fatalities have taken place in the United States and Puerto Rico.

This book presents a lucid analysis of half a century of terrorism in the United States. It highlights the remarkable diversity of US terrorists focusing on white and black racists, Islamic fundamentalists, revolutionary leftists, right-wing extremists, Puerto Rican *independistas*, militant Jews, and anti-abortionists.

Although he notes that the number of loners appears to be growing, Hewitt rejects the popular view that terrorist movements in the United States have in general tended to be small and isolated, offering instead a broader explanation. Holding that membership of social networks provides an important sense of legitimacy and support, he argues that a resort to violence is most likely when members of groups have their hopes and aspirations raised, but then become disillusioned with the political process. Other factors which can trigger the move from holding extremist views to actually engaging in violence include the decline of social movements, and splits within more organized groups.

In addition to the definitional and theoretical contributions, this book is based on a comprehensive dataset of American terrorists, thereby making it invaluable for any scholar in the field. Perhaps unsurprisingly, it shows that the majority of terrorists are aged between 18 and 30, while few are over 50. More intriguingly, the study reveals that many terrorists do not come from poor backgrounds, or are suffering from some form of socioeconomic grievance: indeed, the revolutionary left-wing Weathermen consisted mainly of activists from privileged backgrounds. Moreover, contrary to popular myths, only a handful of terrorists have personality disorders, or exhibit unusual social characteristics: for example, the proportion of terrorists who are married is close to the national average.

Hewitt also critically analyzes the counter-terrorist actions of the US government. Particularly after the Oklahoma and WTC attacks the US Congress gave increasing powers to the FBI, while the federal government has adopted a more pro-active policy aimed at preventing terrorist attacks. The main "targets" have been the domestic extreme right and Islamic fundamentalists. There has also been growing activity in recent years from NGOs such as the Anti-defamation League and the Southern Poverty Law Center. The latter has used common law principles successfully to bring suits against white separatist organizations in particular on behalf of victims of racial attacks.

Hewitt notes that terrorism has almost always been a failure. Even the September 11 attacks have hardly affected the basic American socioeconomic or political system, or key policies such as support for Israel (the United States may have sought to exert greater pressure in this sphere, but its results appear to have been minimal). However, Hewitt stresses that there have been growing infringements on civil liberties in the "land of the free" since these major attacks. Further major al Qaeda attacks could prompt even greater state intervention (they could also seriously affect world business confidence). Moreover, it is important not to focus unduly on Islam. America's domestic extreme right is greatly angered both by growing state control and by continuing US support for Israel. Animal rights groups too appear to be taking on a more violent hue.

This book is, therefore, both highly authoritative and timely.

Roger Eatwell and Cas Mudde
Bath and Antwerp

Preface

This book is about terrorism in America. Until very recently, most Americans thought of the United States as a land without terrorism – or at least without *serious* terrorism. In fact, there has been a lot of terrorism in America over the last fifty years, some of it by foreigners, but most of it by Americans.

In understanding any social phenomenon, good data are important and the more data the better. A simple analysis of good data is to be preferred to a sophisticated analysis of poor data. This book is based on a chronology of over 3,000 terrorist incidents, which allows a comparative analysis of nine waves of terrorism during the 1954–2000 period. Additional information on over 700 terrorism-related fatalities (victims and terrorists) was also collected, as were data on the captures, arrests, and trials of those engaging in terrorism.

At the beginning of September 2001, I had an almost completed manuscript about American terrorism. Then, like millions of others, I watched on television as the horrifying events of September 11 unfolded. The first chapter describes the political and social impacts of the September 11 attack, and the way that the media interpreted the attack. One common journalistic view was that this terrorism represented something completely new, and that it could be explained as a manifestation of "extremism." Although the scale of the attack was unprecedented, the perception that terrorism was a novelty reveals a certain ignorance of American history. Therefore the second chapter provides an historical overview of terrorism in America, as well as examining the concept of extremism. The third chapter examines the political context of each of the nine waves of terrorism: government policies, public opinion, and support for extremism. The fourth chapter looks at the relationship between extremist movements and the emergence of terrorism, and describes the organizational dynamics of terrorist groups. Chapter 5 analyzes the social and psychological characteristics of the terrorists themselves, and chapter 6 discusses the government's response – in particular how law enforcement and the criminal justice system have dealt with terrorism. Chapter 7 looks at the consequences of American terrorism, its economic, social and political impacts. In the final chapter some predictions about the future are made, and some suggestions about counterterrorism policy are offered. The manuscript was completed by the beginning of December, and except for minor changes suggested by the editors and other readers, I have left it unchanged.

Several people have read and commented on the manuscript, and I would like to thank John Finn, William Rothstein, Ann Schnare, Eric Willenz, as well as the editors of the series, Cas Mudde and Roger Eatwell, for their insightful suggestions. The responsibility for any remaining errors, and of course for the opinions expressed, is entirely mine. I dedicate the book to the women in my life: my wife Maire, and my daughters, Sara and Victoria.

C.H.

1   The latest atrocity

On Tuesday, September 11, 2001, terrorists hijacked four planes filled
with passengers. At 8:48 a.m. the first plane crashed into the north
tower of the World Trade Center in New York City. Fifteen minutes
later the second plane flew into the south tower. Both towers burst
into flames and later collapsed. Shortly before 10:00 a.m., the third
plane crashed into the Pentagon outside Washington DC. The fourth
plane crashed in rural Pennsylvania, after passengers attacked the
hijackers.[1]

The attacks were unprecedented in terms of the number of deaths,
and the amount of damage which resulted. In addition to the 226
passengers on the four planes (including the nineteen hijackers),
almost 3,000 persons lost their lives at the World Trade Center and
125 people perished at the Pentagon.[2] Preliminary estimates of the
costs of the physical damage alone suggested that they would be over
$5 billion. The attacks were certain to be the worst insurance disaster
in history, with analysts saying that the total for all claims could run
as high as $40 billion (Treastor 2001).

The American response was also unprecedented. All commercial air
traffic was grounded for two days. Aircraft carriers and destroyers
armed with surface-to-air missiles were stationed in the coastal
waters off California and New York. Fighter jets patrolled the skies
over Washington and New York, and soldiers stood guard in down-
town areas.

The Justice Department launched "the most massive and intensive investigation ever conducted in America," according to Attorney
General Ashcroft, with 4,000 FBI agents assigned to the case. Within
a few days, the nineteen hijackers were identified, and linked with the
radical Islamic network of Osama bin Laden. They ranged in age
from twenty to forty-one, with most being in their mid-twenties.
Most were Saudis, but one was Lebanese and two were from the

United Arab Emirates, while the apparent leader, Mohammed Atta, was Egyptian. The hijackers did not fit the suicide bomber profile found in previous research on Middle Eastern terrorists (Wilgoren 2001). They were educated; in some cases they had spent years in the United States; at least one was married with children. As Brian Jenkins, a terrorism expert with the Rand Corporation, noted:

> What is extraordinary about this episode is that these people were preparing for their mission for months, leading normal lives with wives, taking the garbage out, taking their kids to McDonalds, taking flying lessons, living in comparatively pleasant places, all the while knowing that at some future date they were going to kill themselves and thousands of people.[3]
>
> (DeYoung *et al.* 2001: A8)

They lived middle-class lives, and aroused no suspicion among their neighbors. This ability to pass was, of course, helped by the growing diversity within much of America. As a *New York Times* article (Golden *et al.* 2001) noted:

> Although some of them spoke little English, they barely stood out in a landscape that has grown increasingly diverse. . . . Florida turned out to be a fine place for a terrorist to train. The polyglot racial mix, the transient culture of rental apartments, the simple procedures for getting a driver's license.

The terrorists entered the United States legally. Fifteen received business or tourist visas, while one had a vocational education visa – allowing him to train as a pilot.

The Osama bin Laden network, known as al Qaeda (the base), is composed of radical Muslim groups operating in at least thirty-five countries. Apparently an infrastructure of supporters has existed in the United States since the early 1990s, and includes "sleeper cells" that can be activated for specific attacks. Following the September 11 attacks almost 1,200 Muslims were arrested as material witnesses or detained for immigration violations, the largest such operation since World War II. The detentions were apparently intended to thwart potential attacks by al Qaeda, and most of those detained had no obvious links to the hijackers ("Deliberate strategy of disruption" 2001).

Osama bin Laden and his followers see themselves as fighting a *jihad* (or holy war) against the United States. In 1998 bin Laden said:

"To kill Americans and their allies – civilians and military – is an individual duty for every Muslim." Previous attacks on American targets attributed to the group include the 1993 bombing of the World Trade Center, the 1996 bombing of a US military complex in Dhahran, Saudi Arabia, the 1998 bombing of US embassies in Kenya and Tanzania, and the bombing of the USS *Cole* in Aden in 2000. In December 1999, an Algerian linked to the group was arrested at the Canadian border with bomb-making materials in his car.

Social and economic impacts

Almost all major sports and cultural events were canceled in the aftermath of the tragedy. The National Football League announced that it would not hold any of the games scheduled for the weekend, and Major League Baseball, the PGA tour, auto racing and other sports followed suit. The three television networks postponed the start of their fall season premieres for a week, while the Emmy Awards, the Latin Grammy Awards, and New York fashion shows were canceled indefinitely. Television and cinema executives quickly replaced films involving explosions and hijackings with patriotic stories, family dramas and escapist comedies. One executive announced that the entertainment being offered would be "much more wholesome with movies reinforcing American values, family and community" (Weinraub 2001).

The indirect economic costs are difficult to calculate precisely but were certainly significant. For days, American business was paralyzed, many stores closed, and sales were down sharply in those that remained open. Hardest hit was the airline industry, which was already in bad financial straits. The major airlines announced layoffs and warned that they might file for bankruptcy protection. As passengers canceled their flight plans a ripple effect was felt throughout other sectors of the travel industry, including hotels, resorts, convention centers, cab and auto rental companies. The insurance industry and financial markets suffered heavy losses. Following fears that terrorists might use crop-duster planes to spread toxic chemicals or deadly diseases, the planes were grounded. Not only did this take away the livelihoods of about 5,000 pilots but farmers feared their crops would suffer (Canedy 2001). The stock market was closed for the rest of the week, but after they reopened the Dow Jones average plunged 1,370 points (14.3 percent) in the week – the worst decline ever. Analysts predicted that the attack would tip the economy into recession as consumer confidence plunged.[4]

The public mood

The public mood went from panic to patriotism. When schools and offices closed there was some initial panic in Washington DC, leading to massive traffic jams as people fled the city, but this was followed by a surge of patriotism. American flags appeared everywhere, outside homes, on cars, on bridges, as did signs saying "God bless America," "Pray for America," or "United we stand." So many Americans donated blood that the nation's chronic shortage disappeared temporarily, with blood bank inventories tripling in a week (Goldstein 2001). A television fund-raiser for the families of those killed or injured generated more than $150 million in pledges.

Following the attacks, people thought to be Arabs or Muslims were threatened, harassed, and assaulted. The Council on American–Islamic Relations received several hundred reports of anti-Muslim incidents from around the country. In Arizona, a gunman shot to death the Sikh owner of a gas station, then fired at a Lebanese clerk working in a nearby gas station, and at a home owned by an Afghan family. In New York, a man tried to run over a Pakistani woman. Mosques were firebombed in Chicago, Cleveland, Seattle, Denton TX, and Smithtown NY. In Cleveland, a man crashed his car through the doors of the Islamic Center, causing $100,000 damage. Because of their turbans and beards, Sikhs were often targets, with over 200 incidents being reported against them, including three arson attacks against Sikh temples. The violence was condemned by President Bush, and by Attorney General Ashcroft, while the Senate passed a resolution calling for the protection of the civil rights and civil liberties "of all Americans including Arab Americans and American Muslims." Nevertheless, the violence reflected widespread suspicion towards Arabs and Muslims. One public opinion poll found that 43 percent of those surveyed reported that they were "personally more suspicious of people of Arab descent" (Edsall 2001a). Another poll found that 58 percent backed more intensive security checks for Arabs (including US citizens), while 49 percent favored special identification cards, and 32 percent wanted special surveillance of them (Verhovek 2001).

A *New York Times* poll found overwhelmingly support for military retaliation against the terrorists, even if "many thousands of innocent people" were killed. A majority were ready to accept some inconvenience in return for increased safety, saying that they would be ready to arrive three hours early for domestic flight security checks, and to pass through metal detectors in public buildings (Berke and Elder 2001). In a survey by *USA Today*, there was similar strong support for military retaliation, even if it required the use of ground troops, and the death of a thousand soldiers, or if it resulted in increased taxes, and oil and gas shortages. The *USA Today* poll also found that large majorities favored increased security in airports and public places (Memmott 2001).

The political response

Tuesday's events were so catastrophic that security considerations dictated that the President should leave Washington until it was determined that he could safely return. Thus it was not until the evening that Bush addressed the nation. In a short four-minute speech he told the American people that "thousands of lives were suddenly ended by evil, despicable acts of terror" and vowed that the United States would hunt down and punish those responsible. "These acts of mass murder were intended to frighten our nation into chaos and retreat but they have failed," he declared. In the days following, the President visited the site of the attacks, and attended a prayer service at the National Cathedral in Washington. On Thursday 20th, in a speech to a joint session of Congress, Bush demanded that the Taliban government of Afghanistan turn over Osama bin Laden, and close all terrorist training camps in that country. "Our war on terror," he said "will not end until every terrorist group of global reach has been found, stopped, and defeated," but he warned that it would be a long campaign. Bush declared that any country that harbored or supported terrorists would be regarded as a hostile regime. He emphasized several times that the enemy was not Islam[5] or the Arabs. "Our enemy is a radical network of terrorists and every government that supports them."

In its campaign against terrorism, the Bush administration adopted a multifaceted strategy. On the military side, warships were deployed to the Persian Gulf and Special Force units to Afghanistan. On October 8, American and British planes began bombing Kabul, Jalalabad, and Kandahar, the three largest towns. On the diplomatic front, the United States sought successfully to build a broad coalition against terrorism. The United Arab Emirates severed relations with Afghanistan, and Pakistan and Iran sealed their borders. Russia announced that it would share intelligence with the United States, and allow American planes to overfly its air space. Arguing that "money is the lifeblood of terrorist operations," President Bush froze the assets of all suspected Islamic terrorist groups in the United States. More important, the Treasury Secretary was given broad powers to impose sanctions on foreign financial institutions if they did not cooperate in sharing information about suspected terrorist accounts and funding (Sanger and Kahn 2001). The anti-Taliban coalition within Afghanistan, the Northern Alliance, was supplied with weapons and supported by American air power. By late December, the Taliban had been overthrown and US special forces were searching caves along the Pakistan border for Osama bin Laden and other al Qaeda leaders.

At least initially, the attack produced a show of bipartisanship and cooperation between Democrats and Republicans. By a vote of 98–0 in the Senate and 420–1 in the House, Congress passed a joint resolution authorizing President Bush to use "all necessary and appropriate force" against those involved in the attack.[6] Congress also voted $40 billion in emergency spending to cover the cost of rebuilding and increased security. Another $15 billion to bail out the struggling airline industry was approved with large bipartisan majorities. Prior to the terrorist attack, the political scene had been marked by bitter wrangling over social security and disagreement over some of the Bush nominees for federal positions. In the aftermath of the attack, controversial nominations were withdrawn, and debates on such potentially divisive issues as a patients' bill of rights and the anti-missile defense system were postponed.

The need to display national unity at a time of crisis may have muted political debate, but political divisions did not disappear in Congress or the wider society. Rather the new situation helped some special interests while it disadvantaged others, and led to new alliances between old adversaries. The AFL-CIO and the US Chamber of Commerce jointly announced their support for major public investments to provide a stimulus to the weakened economy. Equally striking was the shared opposition by both conservative and liberal groups to the threat of increased government surveillance and expanded police powers. The conservative Free Congress Foundation and the Gun Owners of America held a news conference together with the liberal American Civil Liberties Union and the Leadership Conference on Civil Rights to voice their concern that the new initiatives would threaten individual rights and privacy (Edsall 2001b).

The uneasy compromise between national unity and partisan disagreement was most evident in the final form of the anti-terrorism bill. Agreement was reached only after days of tense negotiations between Democrats and the Bush administration (Lancaster 2001). The bill expanded the ability of law enforcement and intelligence agencies to wiretap phones and monitor internet messages. A single court order would authorize "roving wiretaps" under which investigators could tap any phone used by a suspected terrorist. Law enforcement and intelligence agencies were allowed to share grand jury and wiretap transcripts. However, an administration proposal under which non-citizens suspected of terrorist offences could be jailed indefinitely was dropped. Instead suspects could be detained for only seven days, after which they would have to be charged or released. The bill passed the Senate unanimously, and the House by a vote of 357 to 66.

The fact that the attacks had been perpetrated by foreigners led to calls for tighter immigration controls. Rep. Lamar Smith, a member of the House immigration subcommittee, declared that "We're going to have to do a better job of making sure we know who comes into the country, how long they're supposed to be here, and whether they've left or not." The new concerns appear to have stopped, at least temporarily, proposals by the Bush administration to grant amnesty to millions of illegal immigrants (Sheridan 2001).

The media: interpreting the atrocity

The terrorist attacks dominated the media for weeks, as viewers watched the traumatic events unfold in horrifying detail. The round-the-clock television coverage broke the previous record set after the assassination of President Kennedy in November 1963, when CBS and NBC stayed on the air with continuous news reports for four days. Certain themes – such as the appalling death toll, and the heroism of firefighters, police, and emergency workers – were emphasized again and again. It was once cynically claimed that "ten deaths is a tragedy, a thousand is a statistic," but in their reporting the media personalized the tragedy, as the dead and missing were identified. Photographs of the victims, often with detailed descriptions, were published in local newspapers, showing them as mothers and fathers, co-workers, friends and neighbors. Accounts of those who had escaped reinforced the message that this horror could have happened to any of the readers. A typical story in the *New York Times* (Walsh 2001) described the experiences of "two ordinary people among the thousands caught in the World Trade Center on Tuesday morning."

But who was responsible, and why had they done this terrible thing? How should we respond, and what could be done to stop other attacks? The editorials and opinion writers offered a variety of responses to these questions. Initially, most expressed anger and incomprehension. The day after the attack, the lead editorial in the *New York Times* was headed "An Unfathomable Attack." Before the attack Americans had believed "that there were some things that no human being would want to do . . . consider the intensity of the hatred it took to bring it off.

It is a hatred that exceeds the conventions of warfare, that knows no limits, abides by no agreements."

Suspicion quickly fell on Osama bin Laden and his network, usually described as "Islamic fundamentalists" or "Muslim radicals," although a number voiced suspicions that one or more Arab governments were responsible. William Safire (2001a) asked, "What well-financed terrorist organization under what country's secret protection slaughtered so many Americans?" There were, however, conflicting interpretations of *why* they had carried out the attack. Several writers noted that bin Laden himself had explained his grievances against America in a *fatwa* issued in February 1998. The United States was occupying Saudi Arabia and its holy places (Mecca and Medina), was enforcing sanctions against Iraq, and was supporting Israel in its oppression of the Palestinian people. As one writer pointed out: "These complaints require no elaboration in the fatwa; they are immediately understood by the statement's intended Muslim audience" (Hashmi 2001).

Most commentators preferred a more general explanation. The terrorists were attacking America because of its values. "They did it solely out of grievance and hatred – hatred for the values cherished in the West as freedom, tolerance, religious pluralism and universal suffrage" (Schmemann 2001). Joel Achenbach (2001) saw the terrorists as "opposed to all things American, to capitalism, to democracy, to civilization." One of the values of America that he singles out is cultural diversity. "Cultural diversity isn't trivial to us. This is what *we* believe in [his italics]."

Since the terrorists were Muslims, and since they had attacked the United States because it holds Western values, this might suggest that the attack resulted from a clash of civilizations. Indeed Samuel Huntingdon's book, *The Clash of Civilizations and the Remaking of World Order* (1996) argues that future conflicts will be along such cultural fault lines – primarily religious in origin. However, his thesis was cited (somewhat hesitantly) by only a handful of commentators (Tolson 2001). Several commentators went out of their way to assure their readers that Muslims and the Muslim world were not the enemy.[7]

The most popular interpretation saw "fundamentalism" and "fundamentalists" as the underlying enemy. Thomas Friedman (2001a) argued that "The real clash today is actually not between civilizations but within them – between those Muslims, Christians, Hindus, Buddhists and Jews with a modern and progressive outlook and those with a medieval one." According to John Leo (2001) "this is a global cultural war, pitting a pan-Islamic movement of fundamentalist extremists against the modern world and its primary cultural engine, America, the Great Satan. But this does not mean that, we are in a battle against Islam." The equation of modernism with America is made repeatedly. George Will (2001) explained that: "The soldiers of militant Islam . . . hate America because it is the purest expression of modernity – individualism, pluralism, freedom, secularism." Salman Rushdie (2001) offered "a brief list" of what fundamentalists are against in modern societies: "freedom of speech, a multiple-party political system, universal adult suffrage, accountable government, Jews, homosexuals, women's rights, pluralism, secularism, short skirts, dancing, beardlessness, evolution theory, sex."

As to what should be done in response to the attacks, the media offered both general and specific suggestions. Most accepted that military action would be necessary, although a minority proposed to rely upon international law. Although calling for increased security in general, and increased airport security in particular, it was stressed that civil liberties must not be abridged unnecessarily. The inability of the FBI and CIA to prevent the attacks was criticized, and the need for intelligence reforms was emphasized. The media were unanimous in condemning the attacks on American Muslims, and rejected any "profiling" of the Muslim community by law enforcement. The Rev. Jerry Falwell, a fundamentalist Protestant minister, was denounced for expressing the view that the attack was a sign of God's displeasure at abortionists, feminists, gays, and lesbians, and the American Civil Liberties Union. Only a few argued for humanitarian aid to improve standards of living in poor countries.[8] In Table 1.1 the themes of the editorials and columnists in the *New York Times, Washington Post, Baltimore Sun, US News & World Report, Time*, and *Newsweek*, are shown for the four-week period after September 11. The figures refer to the percentage of editorials and columnists who mentioned the specified topic. (Since some mentioned more than one topic, the total is more than 100 percent.) The table therefore provides a rough measure of the concerns of opinion leaders, before the first air strikes were launched against Afghanistan, and before the anthrax terrorism scare.

One view expressed again and again, on talk shows and op-ed pages, was that the attack had created a national psychological trauma by exposing US vulnerability. Writing in the *New York Times*, Ronald Steel (2001) declared, "This is the end: the end of an era, the era of our invulnerability," and Frank Rich (2001a) repeated the theme: "We live in a different America today than the day before Tuesday . . .

Table 1.1 Selected themes in editorials and opinion columns after September 11 (% mentioning)

Cause of attack	
Osama bin Laden guilty	16.2
Suspect involvement of Arab state(s)	7.8
US support for Israel	6.0
US troops in Saudi Arabia	3.6
US blockade of Iraq	0.9
Hostility to US values	5.2
Fundamentalism	8.3
Clash of civilizations	1.4
Not US support for Israel	6.9
Not clash of civilizations/Muslim religion	10.1
Poverty and inequality	3.2
Policy suggestions	
Preserve civil liberties	11.1
Support military response	13.2
Improve airport security/immigration control	11.0
Investigate terrorist financing	3.6
Criticize CIA, FBI	10.2
Criticize Rev. Falwell	5.4
Condemn attacks on US Muslims/profiling	16.1
Dangers of bio-terrorism	4.6

We have lost our illusion of impregnability." In the *Baltimore Sun,* Michael Ollove (2001) began his article by saying, "No longer can we tell ourselves that we are safe simply because we live in the United States."

Notes

1 The plane was presumably going for a Washington area target, such as the White House, the Capitol, or Camp David. Terrorists may have plotted to take over two additional flights.
2 The number killed at the World Trade Center was originally estimated at over 6,000. However, many victims were double-counted because they were reported missing by more than one relative or friend, or listed under variant spellings of their names.
3 It is possible that not all the hijackers knew that they were on a suicide mission. One account suggests a division between the pilots and the "soldiers" who acted as "muscle" ("Hijackers had a careful strategy of brains, muscle and practice" 2001).
4 The consumer sentiment index, which was 91.5 in August, dropped sharply to 81.8 in September. The director of the survey said, "A recession is no

longer in doubt, the only issue is how long the downturn will last" (Berry 2001).

5 Unfortunately, the original code name for the US military operation, "Infinite Justice," was offensive to Muslims on the grounds that only God can mete out infinite justice, and had to be changed. Bush was also criticized for insensitivity in talking of a "crusade" against Muslim extremists, since the word also has negative historical connotations for Arabs and Muslims.

6 The sole dissenting vote was by Barbara Lee, a black Democrat, who represented one of the most liberal districts in California. The congresswoman was later given a police bodyguard after receiving death threats.

7 William Safire (2001b) voiced mild criticism: "Why are the voices of revered mainstream Muslim clerics not denouncing the perversion of Islam by the terrorists?"

8 Usually those writing for the *New York Times* and the *Washington Post* emphasize poverty and injustice as the root cause of terrorism but this was rarely mentioned as a factor in the September 11 attacks. The exceptions included the *Washington Post*'s two black columnists. Courtland Milloy (2001) suggested that the root causes of terrorism lay in the global suffering "which is systemic and deeply rooted – in colonialism, racism, religious bigotry and greed." William Raspberry (2001) thinks that "while the seeds of terrorism may have any number of sources (Osama bin Laden is hardly reacting out of grinding poverty), they find their nurture in the fertile ground of despair."

2 Before September 11

American terrorism since the 1950s

The amount of media attention directed to the issue of domestic terrorism has increased dramatically since the early 1990s, and a whole cottage industry has grown up devoted to exposing the dangers from domestic right-wing and Islamic extremists. Yet most of the discussion has lacked any historical perspective. Although the terrorist attack of September 11 caused more death and destruction than any previous incident, the claim that Americans had – overnight – become aware of their vulnerability to a terrorist attack is absurd. Indeed, identical claims were made in 1993 and in 1995. After the 1993 World Trade Center bombing, *Newsweek* (March 8, 1993) declared that the explosion had "rattled the country's confidence, dispelling the snug illusion that Americans were immune, somehow, to the plague of terrorism that torments so many foreign countries." Only two years later, *Newsweek* appeared equally surprised by the Oklahoma City bombing. The headline was "This doesn't happen here," and the first paragraph read: "It looked like Beirut. But the devastated building was deep in America's heartland, ending forever the illusion that here at home we are safe" (May 1, 1995: 26).

It appears to be the conventional wisdom that in America, until recently, terrorism was infrequent and unimportant. In fact, in the past half-century, the United States has experienced a significant amount of terrorism. According to my count, since 1954 but before September 11, well over 3,000 terrorist incidents and more than 700 terrorism-related fatalities have taken place within the United States and Puerto Rico. Certainly the United States has suffered relatively less from terrorist attacks than other Western nations such as Spain, Israel, Italy, or the United Kingdom, but it would be a serious misreading of the historical record to see terrorism as either a new or a trivial phenomenon in America.

However, American terrorism does have two distinctive features. First, there is remarkable ideological diversity among American terrorists. Attacks have been carried out by white and black racists, black nationalists, Islamic fundamentalists, black Muslims, revolutionary communists, neo-Nazis, Puerto Rican *independistas*, Chicano nationalists, militant Jews, anti-abortionists and a variety of *émigré* groups. Second, these ideological groupings are themselves divided into numerous organizations and factions. Furthermore a large number of attacks have been carried out by lone individuals apparently unaffiliated to any organization. It is, one suspects, this confusing and fragmented quality possessed by American terrorism that makes every terrorist incident seem *de novo*.

Definitions and data sets

Analyzing American terrorism is difficult for two interrelated reasons. There is considerable ambiguity as to what should be considered terrorism and there are no reliable official statistics on terrorist incidents. According to White (1991: 163), "the lack of a social or legal definition creates problems. . . . American police and security agencies literally do not know what terrorism is . . . [and] agencies charged with countering domestic terrorism often have no idea what they are looking for."

The pioneering study of post-war violence in the United States is Marcia McKnight Trick's chronology, which covers the period from 1965 to 1976, and was published as an appendix to the report of the Task Force on Disorders and Terrorism (NACCJSG 1976). Trick includes in her chronology:

> incidents in which it would appear that violence to property or persons has been used or threatened for political purposes. Political purposes should be interpreted to include a wide variety of motivations from attempts to influence a government or group's policy to competition for leadership within a group. When these purposes appear to be clearly articulated and adhered to by a particular group, and incidents occur frequently enough to constitute a campaign, such incidents can be characterized as terroristic.

Trick distinguishes between terrorism, "quasi-terrorism," and spontaneous eruptions of violence such as the urban riots of the 1960s. Although the distinction between spontaneous violence and terrorism is an important one there seems little point in restricting terrorism to a series of acts carried out by a group. First, individuals such as the unabomber engage in exactly the same kinds of actions as groups and for motives which are undeniably political. Second, it is often unclear whether a given act was perpetrated by an individual or a group.

This study uses the FBI's definition of terrorism as "the unlawful use of force or violence against persons or property to intimidate or coerce a government, the civilian population, or any segment thereof, in furtherance of political or social objectives." The FBI statistics which begin in 1980 are described by Ross (1993: 111) as "problematic" since they fail to include many incidents of politically motivated violence, such as abortion clinic bombings. Although the FBI formalized its definition of terrorism in 1986, local law enforcement agencies are not required to abide by the definition, and many terrorist actions are misclassified as common crimes (White 1991: 163). Smith (1994) points out that the FBI is reluctant to include an incident in its statistics unless some group claims responsibility.

The analysis is based on three data sets. To measure terrorist activity, I have compiled a chronology beginning in 1954, that incorporates the material contained in Trick's chronology, the *Annual of Power and Conflict*, and the FBI annual reports, and supplements these data with information from newspapers, magazines, and other published sources. The chronology contains information on over 3,000 terrorist incidents. A second chronological listing provides more detail on over 700 terrorism-related fatalities (victims and terrorists). A third data set contains information on arrests, trials, and trial outcomes of those engaging in terrorism. Details on the sources and coding procedures are given in an appendix.

Patterns of terrorism in the United States

Using both incident data and fatalities allows the rise and fall of different types of terrorism to be measured with precision. Terrorism is usually classified in terms of the characteristics of the terrorists: domestic or foreign, leftists or rightists. Domestic terrorism is carried out by American terrorists, foreign terrorism by non-American terrorists. The distinction between American and non-American is sometimes uncertain. In this study, it is assumed that foreign-born individuals (even if naturalized) are non-American, as are American-born mercenaries carrying out terrorist acts on behalf of foreign groups or governments. Puerto Rican nationalist terrorists, although legally US citizens, do not consider themselves as such and so are defined as non-American. Foreign terrorism falls into two types, *émigré* and international, depending on whether the target is American or foreign.

Emigré terrorism, in which a foreign victim is attacked within the United States by a foreign terrorist group, generally involves issues which lie outside American society and politics. To take an extreme example, the Armenian who shot and killed two Turkish diplomats on January 27, 1973, in California was taking revenge for events which occurred during World War I in the Ottoman empire. The most important example of *émigré* terrorism is that involving anti-Castro Cubans, but attacks have also been carried out by Haitians, Sikhs, Taiwanese, Vietnamese, Croatians, Chileans, Iranians, Libyans, Nicaraguans, Palestinians, and Venezuelans. Agents of foreign governments were involved in several instances.[1] *International terrorism*, in which foreign terrorists attack American targets, has been carried out by two groups; Puerto Rican *independistas* and Islamic extremists.

Since both types of foreign terrorism combined account for only 20.3 percent of incidents and 11.6 percent of deaths prior to September 11, it is clear that domestic terrorism is – or was – a more important phenomenon. Classified by ideological type, most domestic terrorism has been carried out by white racists, black militants, and revolutionary leftists. Minor campaigns, on a smaller scale, were conducted by the Jewish Defense League and by anti-abortionist extremists.

There is not a particularly close correspondence between the number of incidents carried out by different types of groups and the fatalities resulting from them. Revolutionary leftists, for example, account for

Table 2.1 Terrorist incidents and fatalities by those responsible, 1954–2000 (%)

Type of terrorism	Incidents	Fatalities
Foreign		
Cuban *émigré*	5.2	1.5
Puerto Rican	11.9	4.3
Islamic	1.1	1.7
Other foreign	2.1	4.1
Domestic terrorism		
White racist/Rightist[a]	31.2	51.6
Revolutionary left	21.2	2.0
Black militants	14.7	25.0
Anti-abortionist	6.2	0.9
Jewish	3.6	0.8
Other domestic/unknown	2.8	8.1
(Total)	(3,228)	(661)

Note
[a] Includes Oklahoma City bombing (168 fatalities).

a large proportion of attacks, but only a small proportion of fatalities. Black militants, on the other hand, are responsible for a greater proportion of fatalities than of attacks. The discrepancy between the two measures may reflect the probability that non-lethal attacks may go unrecorded. Violence by white racists is probably more closely monitored than that by black racists. More important are differences in the tactics employed. Revolutionary leftists typically bombed property, often selecting their targets for symbolic reasons rather than with the intention of killing people.

American terrorism has occurred in a series of waves (as shown in Figure 2.1), reflecting the waxing and waning of campaigns by different groups. Nine waves will be examined in this study. These include all the important cases, which together account for the great majority of terrorist incidents and fatalities during the post-war period prior to the events of September 11.[2] A brief description of the nine cases follows, in rough chronological order.

1. The School Desegregation decision of 1954, and the civil rights campaigns in the 1960s, provoked a violent response from white racists. A resurgent Klan bombed and shot at civil rights activists in an attempt

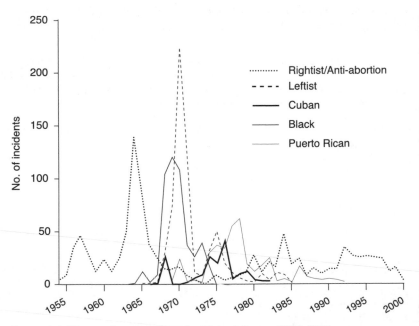

Figure 2.1 Waves of terrorism in the United States, 1954–2000

to intimidate blacks from exercising their rights. The violence began in 1954, peaked in 1964 and was largely over by 1970. A total of 588 incidents (including bombings, shootings, assaults and cases of intimidation), were reported in southern states during this period. There were sixty-five fatalities.

2. Since the mid-1960s, two different types of black groups have carried out violent acts: separatist black religious cults such as the Nation of Islam, and black nationalists such as the Black Panthers. Black separatist cults resorted to violence somewhat later than the black nationalists. The two types of groups engaged in very different forms of violence. Black nationalists carried on a virtual guerrilla war against the police, and killed one another in factional feuds. Black separatist cults, such as the Death Angels and the Mau Mau, murdered randomly selected whites, as well as dissidents and apostates. A total of 475 incidents are recorded; a majority (72 percent) were shooting incidents, but there were scores of bombings and several assaults, robberies, escapes and attempted escapes, and skyjackings. The proportion of deadly incidents was high, with almost 400 killed and wounded in violence involving black militants.

3. Revolutionary leftist groups, such as the Weather Underground, turned to terrorism in 1969; their attacks peaked in 1971, and then declined erratically. The most common type of incident was bombing (over 500 incidents), but in addition leftist terrorists were responsible for at least thirty-seven robberies, ten shootings, a kidnaping, and a prison escape. They rarely attacked individuals, and mostly bombed military and business targets.

4. *Independistas*, Puerto Ricans desiring independence from the United States, resorted to violence in the 1950s[3] and again after 1969. The second wave of terrorism began in 1969, peaked in the late 1970s and then declined erratically. The two most important groups were the Armed Forces of National Liberation (FALN) and the Macheteros; the former were most active on the US mainland, while the latter's attacks were concentrated in Puerto Rico. A total of 365 bombings, ten shootings, six robberies, and two rocket attacks are recorded. The bombing campaign of the FALN was directed against banks, the corporate headquarters of organizations with economic interests in Puerto Rico, and other symbols of US capitalism and imperialism. As a Rand study (Sater 1981: 5) noted, "historically the *independistas* have tended not to strike at individuals. Indeed given the number of bombings very few people have died." Nevertheless, at least eighteen persons have died as a result of Puerto Rican terrorism.[4] On the island, the Macheteros have attacked and killed American sailors and police.

5. Members of the Jewish Defense League and its splinter groups (Jewish Armed Resistance, Thunder of Zion, Save Our Israel Soil) were responsible for bombing Soviet diplomatic targets and Arab embassies, as well as for several attacks on Arab-American organizations and alleged war criminals. A total of 115 incidents are attributed to these groups (all bombings except for four shootings and several assaults), with the great majority of the attacks taking place in and around New York City. Five people died as a result of JDL bombs.

6. Terrorism by anti-Castro Cuban *émigrés* was at first primarily against targets within Cuba. However, after 1968, attacks were directed against targets within the United States, and against those members of the exile community perceived to be traitors to the Cuban cause.

> To be agnostic on the question of Fidel Castro, let alone to call for a renewed dialogue or an end to the US trade embargo, could be dangerous . . . people had been killed for espousing such views. For all the talk of terrorism in the United States over the previous twenty years, Miami was the only American city to experience any significant domestic terrorism.
>
> (Rieff 1993: 85)

Those who spoke out against terrorism were themselves attacked. (One radio news director lost both legs when a bomb exploded in his car.) From 1968 through the early 1980s, at least 168 incidents and ten murders within the United States can be attributed to Cuban extremists.

In addition to these six historical cases, there are three ongoing terrorist threats facing the United States. Arson and bombings of abortion clinics, which began in 1977, increased significantly in 1984 and again after 1992. In recent years, anti-abortion violence has become more deadly, and six persons have been killed. Far more serious is the violence by the far right, which began ca. 1978 and has resulted in almost 100 deaths (in addition to those resulting from the Oklahoma City bombing). This wave of terrorism differs from that by the southern Klans in the 1950s and 1960s in two respects. First, it is national in scope, and a majority of incidents have taken place *outside* the south. Second, although there is an undoubted continuity between the Klan and contemporary white racism, the Klan itself has played a comparatively minor role. Some themes – such as white supremacy and hostility to the federal government – have been carried over, and ex-Klansmen, like Louis Beam and Glenn Miller, have played a significant role in the new groups. However, the most noticeable feature of this second wave of white racist terrorism is its organizational fragmentation. Among the organizations involved are the Order (Silent Brotherhood), the White People's Party, the Covenant, Sword, and Arm of the Lord, the National Socialist White People's Party, and Posse Comitatus. Skinhead gangs also play a significant role. A striking feature of the post-1978 violence is the role played by serial racist killers.

The threat from Islamic extremists was clear even prior to the September 11 attack. Although responsible for only a handful of incidents, their willingness to attack civilian targets and apparent desire to maximize casualties was revealed by the 1993 bombing of the World Trade Center. The September 11 attack, though the tactics were original, should not be seen as involving a new strategy or new goals. In the final chapter, the prospects of future terrorist attacks from Islamic, right-wing, and anti-abortion extremists will be examined.

Explaining American terrorism

Given the diversity and fragmentary quality of American terrorism, there is a superficial plausibility to Walter Laqueur's view that "terrorist movements are usually small; some very small indeed, and while historians and sociologists can sometimes account for mass movements, the movements of small particles in politics as in physics often defy any explanation" (1977: 80). This view is too pessimistic, and in this book an historical and sociological explanation for the emergence, growth, and decline of terrorist violence will be proposed. Major terrorist campaigns are dependent upon well organized infra-structures and a significant degree of popular support. This is true of the IRA in Northern Ireland, ETA in the Basque provinces of Spain, the Red Brigades in Italy and the Tupamaros of Uruguay. Even much smaller campaigns, such as that of the German Red Army Faction, are dependent upon a (correspondingly smaller) network of supporters. A critical degree of support is necessary to maintain the operational capabilities of the terrorists.

Support for terrorism is linked with the existence of extremist move-ments. Extremism can be defined in three ways: statistically, stylisti-cally, and in terms of societal attitudes (George and Wilcox 1992: 11). If it is assumed that attitudes in general, or on some particular issue, can be arranged on a continuum, then those at the "extremes" – left or right – are extremist in a purely statistical sense, with most of the population in the middle. George and Wilcox (1992: 54–62) themselves favor a definition in terms of style and characterize the extremist style as marked by "self-righteousness, fanaticism, and hatred." Thus it is possible to hold centrist views in a "dogmatic and prejudiced" manner, whereas someone who holds radical views may do so in "an open and tolerant manner" and consequently not be an extremist. They list twenty-two specific characteristics of extremists, including such traits as character assassination, double standards, name calling and labeling, belief in conspiracy theories, a Manichean world view, and an assumption of moral superiority.

The position taken in this study is to see extremism as socially defined. In any society at a given time, certain social and political views are considered normal and acceptable, while others are not. The range of acceptable views may be broad or narrow, and changes over time. Non-mainstream views and beliefs may be thought of as ridiculous, dangerous, or both. To characterize someone as "extremist" is to view him as holding opinions that are beyond the pale, not to be taken seriously, to be mocked or punished. The reader can perform a mental experiment to determine which views would be considered extremist by considering what opinions could *not* be said in a social gathering, and would not be published in a major newspaper.

We can also explore the meaning of extremism in contemporary America by considering the media's interpretation (as described in the previous chapter) of the September 11 terrorist attack. It was generally agreed that America was attacked because of its values. Although the list of what America stands for varied somewhat from writer to writer, there was agreement that American values include democracy, tolerance, freedom (including free speech), pluralism, individualism, and secularism.

But in what sense are these national values?[5] Americans certainly believe in democracy, but to describe them as secular is ridiculous.[6] As every survey shows, America is one of the most religious of all modern societies in terms of both belief and church attendance. The signs that appeared all over the country in response to the events of September 11 manifested not only patriotic but also religious sentiments that would be inconceivable in Britain or Europe. Foreign academics and journalists often express amazement and shock at the religious aspects of American life.

Pluralism, tolerance, and free speech are somewhat ambiguous values. Indeed, they have a paradoxical quality – does one tolerate expressions of intolerance? And how did the media's treatment of Rev. Falwell embody these ideals? Certainly, whatever the values a society holds, it must necessarily regard those values opposed to it as antithetical. Since America's values express "modernity," then "fundamentalists" are therefore extremist because they don't accept these "modernist" values. This applies not only to Muslim fundamentalists abroad, but also to American fundamentalists, as several columnists were quick to point out. Frank Rich (2001b) noted "how Taliban-like America's own homegrown mixture of fundamentalism and politics can be," while others pointed out that "Christian fundamentalists" had bombed abortion clinics.

The fact that what the media regard as American values are not necessarily held by all (or most) Americans becomes clear when more specific issues are involved. According to Joel Achenbach (2001) "cultural diversity isn't trivial to us. This is what *we* believe in [his italics]." But if this is true, then why did 58 percent of those surveyed "think that immigrants should blend into American culture rather than maintain their own culture" according to a June 2001 *Gallup Report*? Salman Rushdie's list of what fundamentalists are against in modern society includes homosexuality and evolution theory. Yet if these are fundamentalist positions, an alarming number of Americans are fundamentalists. According to the most recent polls, a plurality (45 percent) believe that "God created humans pretty much in their present form at one time about ten thousand years ago," and a majority (53 percent) regard homosexuality as "morally wrong" (*Gallup Reports* October, February 2000). What the media describe as American values are in fact the values of the powerful: dominant values rather than national values. The dominant values can be imposed on a society in a variety of ways. In contemporary democracies, governments may censor or punish those advocating certain positions, but usually it is the media and educational institutions that play the major role in determining what is acceptable.

In practice, whichever of the three definitions is adopted, a very similar group of organizations and views will be characterized as extremist. Thus George and Wilcox (1992: 55) acknowledge that extremists mostly advocate "fringe" positions, and their own list of American extremists is identical to what would be produced using the criterion favored here. To understand the emergence of terrorism, it is first necessary to consider what issue positions are excluded from the political arena, which is the subject of the next chapter.

Notes

1 The Chilean regime of Pinochet organized the 1976 car bombing that killed Orlando Letelier and Ronni Moffit in Washington DC. A Chilean court convicted Manuel Contreras, the former chief of the Chilean secret police, of being involved in the murder plot. The Libyan government has been accused of being behind the assassination of Libyan dissidents.

2 The most important omission is the violence that occurred on the Pine
   Ridge reservation between militants of the American Indian Movement
   and supporters of the tribal authorities, in which a score of people died.
   Unfortunately, good information on this case is lacking.
3 In October 1950, the Puerto Rican Nationalist Party launched an island-
   wide revolt in which twenty-seven persons were killed and fifty-one injured.
   In a related incident, a White House guard was killed during an assassination attempt on President Truman. In 1954, a group of Nationalist Party
   members fired on to the floor of the House of Representatives, wounding
   five congressmen.
4 In addition, the FALN was probably responsible for the La Guardia airport bombing of December 1975 which killed eleven people.
5 Compare Seymour Martin Lipset's analysis in *First New Nation* (1963) and
   Continental Divide (1989) of American national values, and how they differ
   from those of other nations. According to Lipset, these distinctive values
   result from America's revolutionary origins. For example, Americans are
   egalitarian, suspicious of authority in general and government in particular,
   in contrast to Canadians, who represent the counterrevolutionary tradition
   of North America.
6 The only truly secular group in the United States are the journalists.
   According to Lichter *et al.* (1986: 22) "A distinctive characteristic of the
   media elite is its secular outlook. Exactly half eschew any religious affiliation. Another 14 percent are Jewish, and almost one in four (23 percent)
   was raised in a Jewish household. . . . Very few are regular churchgoers."

3 The political context of American terrorism

This chapter looks at the political context of terrorism in America. Specifically, it considers government policies on those issues which have provoked terrorism: desegregation, racial equality, the Vietnam war, Puerto Rican independence, Cuba, abortion, etc. In addition, public opinion, organizational memberships, and other indicators are examined to see to what extent terrorists have a constituency – a potential basis of support – for their actions. How many sympathizers are there for violent or extremist groups, and what are their characteristics? These data can be used to test two alternative explanations as to why democratic politics lead to social violence. One view is that citizens resort to violence because their views and interests are ignored by politicians. The other view is that politicians by "pandering" to extremists incite them to violence.

Excluded opinions and extremist violence

Proponents of the view that violence is a response to being excluded from the political arena argue that if people see the political system as responsive to their concerns they will not resort to violence. The existence of terrorism is therefore an indicator of political alienation. This truism implies that, in order to understand terrorism, we must consider whose opinions and interests are being ignored. Pluralists emphasize that a wide variety of opinions and interests are allowed to organize and compete in the political arena, but in practice certain groups and opinions are excluded from the process. Such exclusion may occur for several reasons. Sometimes political cleavages coincide with ascriptive identities and produce permanent minorities, as in Northern Ireland, and other ethnically divided societies. Blacks in the United States were, until recently, disfranchised in many states, and continue to be underrepresented in terms of voting strength, political

power, and influence. Consequently, in so far as political issues have a
racial character, black interests and concerns will often be disregarded.
Another reason why certain positions are excluded from political
debate involves the logic of political competition. In most Western
democracies, political opinions can be seen in terms of a left–right continuum. Electoral competition in a two-party system results in a drive
for the center (Downs 1957). Consequently, those who are at the ideological extremes, Communists and Socialists, Birchers and neo-Nazis,
find themselves ignored.

The exclusion of certain demands from political consideration can be
seen in terms of a continuum. Some views may be defined as completely
"beyond the pale," absurd or even wicked, while others are merely
overlooked. Schmid and de Graaf (1982) consider terrorist violence
as a form of communication, "the outgrowth of minority strategies to
get into the news." Other positions may become the subject of political
debate but fail to get on to the decision-making agenda.

There are various ways of measuring the number of those who feel
alienated from the political system; those who are on the political and
social fringes of American democracy, the extremists. We can look at
public opinion polls, and also at the number who are mobilized in
some form or other. Presumably, the greater the strength of extremist
sentiments, and the greater the number of people who belong to
extremist groups, the more likely it is that terrorism will occur.

Encouraging extremist violence

However, other writers argue that terrorist violence results not from the
fact that politicians ignore certain issues and opinions, but because they
play up and pander to them. Thus Mullins (1993: 155) sees the mid-
1980s as providing "an opportune political environment for the
right-wing terrorist. . . . It did not take long for the far-right to pick
up on the signals being sent by the Washington administration. . . .
Some increases in hate-crime activity can be attributed both to the
recession and the conservative political climate in the country."
Following an attack on an abortion clinic, an editorial in *The Nation*
(January 23, 1995) argued that "John Salvi was no lone gunman. . . .
After twenty years of denunciation of 'baby-killers' from pulpit, Oval
Office and TV studio, it was only a matter of time before someone
took the rhetoric at face value. There were a lot of fingers on Salvi's
trigger." Jesse Jackson blamed the burning of black churches on
those "who use thinly coded, veiled race symbols when they say welfare
and crime and anti-affirmative action. They're sending signals, they're

sending messages more profound than their language . . . they're laying the groundwork for those who burn churches" (Kelly 1996).

These arguments imply that we should find a general pattern whereby, for any particular type of extremist violence, there will be more violence under sympathetic than under hostile administrations. The claim that speeches have effects is plausible, but it is difficult to specify which speeches and why. Speeches by authority figures, such as Presidents, presumably have more effect than those by interest group representatives. The nature of the political rhetoric surrounding each issue could also be significant. In so far as the political debate on an issue involves extremist rhetoric, it is presumably more likely to result in violence.

To test these alternative models, the political context of six historical and three contemporary waves of terrorism are examined. The historical cases are white racist terrorism in the south during the civil rights period, black terrorism in the late 1960s and early 1970s, left-wing terrorism in the 1970s, terrorism by Puerto Rican *independistas*, and two relatively minor campaigns by *émigré* Cubans and militant Jews. The three ongoing cases are terrorism by anti-abortionists, by Islamic militants, and by the extreme right.

White racist terrorism in the south

The existence of a sizable group of "extremists" among white southerners during the civil rights period is undeniable, although one needs to be careful about how the term is defined. While a majority supported segregation, only a minority supported violence. According to Gallup polls, in 1965 4 percent had a highly favorable view of the Klan, compared with 59 percent with a highly unfavorable view. By 1970 opinions were even more negative, with only 6 percent having a highly favorable and 80 percent a highly unfavorable view of the group. Translated into raw numbers this implies that there were about 1,300,000 Klan sympathizers in 1965 and 1,660,000 in 1970.

Klan membership itself is difficult to estimate for obvious reasons. Almost all sources agree, however, that membership increased dramatically in response to civil rights activity, reached a peak in the mid-1960s, and then declined precipitously. The Anti-defamation League estimated the total at 42,000 in 1965, 55,000 in 1967, and a mere 5,000 in 1973.[1] These trends obviously correlate with the rise and fall of racist violence. However, the largest segregationist organization was not the Klan, but the White Citizens' Councils. The councils were middle-class in composition and used economic pressure to resist desegregation efforts. Some estimates as to the total membership of the councils place it at 750,000, but McMillen (1971: 153–4) concludes that "in all probability, the Council in its heyday never had as many as 250,000 members," and that membership declined to 50,000 in 1960, and to just over 20,000 in 1968.

To what extent, if any, did the political context have any observable effect on terrorist violence? None of the presidential administrations during the period can be characterized as pro-segregationist. Eisenhower's civil rights bills of 1957 and 1960 were the first since Reconstruction. He ended segregation in the DC schools, and expressed the hope that this would become a model for other school systems. He took strong action to enforce the desegregation orders of the federal courts, and during the crisis in Little Rock federalized the Arkansas National Guard and sent the 101st Airborne Division to protect black pupils.

Kennedy was an outspoken advocate of school desegregation, although critics complained that his presidential performance did not live up to his campaign promises.[2] Kennedy twice asserted federal power, once against Governor Ross Barnett of Mississippi and once against Governor George Wallace of Alabama. Twenty thousand troops were sent to Mississippi, and both Governor Barnett and Lieutenant Governor Johnson were indicted for criminal contempt of the federal courts when the University of Mississippi was integrated. The Kennedy administration also established a Committee on Equal Employment Opportunity, issued an executive order prohibiting racial discrimination in federally assisted housing, and used the threat of withholding federal funds to encourage school desegregation.

The Johnson administration enacted major civil rights legislation, including the omnibus Civil Rights Act of 1964, the Voting Rights Act of 1965, and the Housing Act of 1968. The Johnson era legislation went far beyond that of previous administrations. For example, the 1968 Housing Act covered 80 percent of all dwellings, compared with the 18 percent affected by Kennedy's executive order. The Voting Rights Act, in effect, enfranchised southern blacks for the first time since Reconstruction.

There were no civil rights initiatives under Nixon, and critics charged that in pursuit of his southern strategy the administration was reluctant to stringently enforce desegregation policies. Civil rights leaders were openly mistrustful, and at the NAACP's 1970 convention one speaker claimed that "for the first time since Woodrow Wilson, we have a national administration that can be rightly characterized as anti-Negro" (Wolk 1971: 232–4). The US Commission on Civil Rights

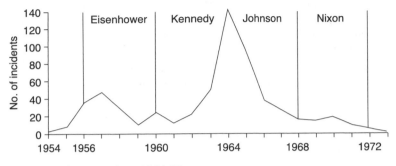

Figure 3.1 Klan terrorism, 1954–72

stated in October 1970 that there was a major breakdown in the enforcement of laws against racial discrimination.

There appears to be no link between the policies of each presidential administration and the amount of violence that occurred. However, since the struggle over segregation was at the same time a struggle over states' rights, it is possible that the state-level political situation was more significant than the national political situation. A study of the southern reaction to desegregation by Sarratt (1966) indicates that the border states generally accepted the 1954 Court decision, but that even in the deep south there were variations in the intensity of the opposition, with Arkansas, Mississippi, Alabama, South Carolina, Louisiana, Georgia, and Virginia being the most uncompromising. Within this group, Mississippi, Alabama, and Arkansas were marked by the intensity of their opposition to desegregation.[3] On the other hand, Governor Collins of Florida and Governor Sanford of North Carolina were noticeably moderate on the issue. "Although a number of Southern governors recognized the legal force of the Brown decision, no other defended the Supreme Court as did LeRoy Collins, governor of Florida," while Sanford's position was "that the courts had settled the question of desegregation and that race was a closed issue in North Carolina politics" (Sarratt 1966: 8, 24–5).

The political rhetoric of the governors paralleled the positions taken by their administrations, and Sarratt (1966: 6–7) singles out Faubus, Wallace, and Barnett for their extremist statements.

Governor Faubus of Arkansas likened the federal courts to the Nazi judiciary under Adolf Hitler. . . . George C. Wallace, governor of Alabama at the decade's end, was especially vitriolic in his attacks on the federal judges, whom he described at various times as "the sorriest in the world," "lousy and irresponsible," "a bunch of atheistic pro-Communist bums," and "bearded beatniks and faceless, spineless, power-hungry theorists and black-robed judicial anarchists." . . . Governor Ross Barnett of Mississippi pledged that he would "rot in a federal jail before he will let one nigra cross the sacred threshold of our white schools."

The variation between the southern states offers the possibility that we can identify the factors that were most significant in affecting the level of violence. In Table 3.1 the states are ranked according to the number of incidents that took place within their borders. In addition, three measures of extremist sentiments are shown for each state. These include an estimate of the number of Klansmen in early 1967, and the combined segregationist vote in the 1960, 1964, and 1968 presidential elections.[4] In the final column, the state response to the desegregation issue is summarized as extreme, strong, or moderate.

Not surprisingly, there is a relationship (although a weak one) between the number of Klansmen and the amount of violence. The correlation ($p > 0.05$) with the statistics on Klan strength given in the 1967 report by the House on un-American activities is 0.48. The report is described as "one of the most detailed and complete studies of the Klan ever undertaken" (George and Wilcox 1992: 398). However, the correlation between the number of segregationist voters and segregationist violence is negligible and statistically insignificant.

The fact that the two most violent states were also the ones in which the governors took extreme positions – even to the extent of defying the

Table 3.1 Segregationist terrorism and state characteristics, 1954–70

State	Incidents	Klan members	Segregationist vote	State response
Mississippi	240	6,030	888,000	Extreme
Alabama	117	1,300	1,351,000	Extreme
Georgia	52	1,580	1,153,000	Strong
Louisiana	38	1,050	1,087,000	Strong
Tennessee	32	275	945,000	Moderate
Florida	30	770	1,530,000	Moderate
N. Carolina	26	7,250	1,121,000	Moderate
Texas	18	200	1,543,000	Moderate
S. Carolina	17	1,050	524,000	Strong
Arkansas	13	255	513,000	Extreme
Virginia	8	1,250	803,000	Strong

courts – could be taken as showing the effect of political leadership on the level of violence. However, the low level of violence in Arkansas, where Faubus engaged in similar brinkmanship with the courts and the federal government, makes this a dubious argument. A more plausible explanation of the correlation between state policies and extremism is put forward by Sarratt, who concluded that "almost without exception, the governors based their positions on the will of the people of their state." In those few cases where governors took a more liberal position than their constituents, they lost to segregationist challengers. Thus Collins in Florida, Folsom in Alabama, and Coleman in Mississippi "failed in bids for re-election against candidates who were more vigorous in their support of segregation." Newspapers had a similar relationship with their readers,[5] and "on the school–race issue, the public seemed to be molding newspaper opinion as much as the newspapers were molding public opinion" (1966: 6, 11, 248).

Black terrorism

The degree of support for black militants can be gauged from several polls. Those favoring a "separate Negro nation" increased from 4 percent in 1963 to 21 percent in 1969. Attitudes towards black leaders and organizations also suggest an increase in nationalist and separatist sentiments, in the late 1960s. Table 3.2 shows the proportion of blacks who rated specified groups or individuals as "doing an excellent job" (Goldman 1970; *Time* April 6, 1970).

Other surveys produced similar results, with 25 percent saying that "the Black Panthers represent my own personal views," and 18 percent giving the Panthers a "highly favorable" rating in a 1970 Gallup poll. These data indicate that support for militant black groups increased sharply in the late 1960s and early 1970s, and that 20–5 percent were

Table 3.2 Favorable attitudes among blacks to black leaders and groups (%)

Leader or group	1963	1966	1969	1970
Stokeley Carmichael	–	7	12	26
Malcolm X	–	–	13	–
Elijah Muhammad	5	4	9	23
Black Panthers	–	–	5	25
Black Muslims	4	4	4	–
Eldridge Cleaver	–	–	–	30
Bobby Seale	–	–	–	23

sympathizers in 1970, which would imply a total of 2 million to 3 million. Since their constituencies were virtually identical, the Black Panthers, the Nation of Islam, and other groups were competing with one another for support.[6] The extent to which potential supporters were mobilized can be measured in several ways. The Nation of Islam grew dramatically in the late 1950s, and throughout the 1960s, reaching a peak of perhaps 250,000 by 1970 (Bowman 1994: 82).[7] The Black Panther Party, founded in 1966, had between 2,000 and 5,000 members in 1968. Another indicator is newspaper readership, which is given as 600,000 for the black Muslim paper (Goldman 1970), and 140,000 for the Black Panther paper (Heath 1976). The figure for the black Muslims is grossly inflated, because members were given a quota and when this was ended sales plummeted to 50,000 (Clegg 1997: 279). Both the public opinion data and the membership statistics show that in the late 1960s and early 1970s, large numbers of blacks were frustrated and alienated. The growth of extremist sentiment and organizations parallels, in a general sense, the outbreak of black violence during the same period.

The political climate in the country at large was increasingly favorable to civil rights and racial equality. Throughout the period, racial issues dominated the political agenda and black grievances and demands were publicized by the media. There is general agreement that greater efforts were made by some administrations than by others. According to Wolk (1971: 239)

> The expressed moral commitment of President Kennedy and the executive civil rights actions taken during his administration appear in sharp contrast to enforcement efforts expended under Eisenhower. Moreover, progress made during Johnson's presidency, especially in the legislative area, far surpassed the accomplishments of all who served in that office before him.

It is very noticeable that most black terrorism occurred during the Nixon administration, when by all accounts civil rights were de-emphasized.

It is possible that the *local* political situation is also a factor in explaining terrorism by black militants. As noted earlier, most black terrorism took place in large cities, and in Table 3.3 the rate of black terrorist incidents (per million blacks) is shown for thirteen of the fifteen largest black communities. (Since no information could be found for two cities, Houston and Dallas, they were not included.) Three cities have noticeably higher rates: San Francisco, New York, and New Orleans. Is there something about the politics of these cities

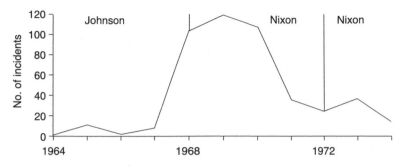

Figure 3.2 Black terrorism, 1964–74

that explains this? Three studies of black political participation were consulted. Patterson (1974) compared the black voting-age population in fourteen cities, ca. 1970, with black representation on the city council. Typically blacks were underrepresented, although there was considerable variation between cities. The Joint Center for Political Studies (1977) lists all cities which had black mayors before 1975, and Browning (1990: 222) ranks twenty-one cities according to the

Table 3.3 Rates of black terrorism and the black political situation, by city

City	Attacks/ million	Black representation (%)	Political situation
San Francisco	326	−3.7	Weak incorporation
New Orleans	139	−39.7	−
New York	93	−9.0	Weak incorporation
Cleveland	59	+4.3	Black mayor
Chicago	51	−0.2	−
Newark	39	−8.6	Black mayor
Atlanta	31	−21.0	Black mayor
Baltimore	31	−17.4	−
Los Angeles	30	n.a.	Black mayor
Detroit	24	−17.2	Black mayor
Washington DC	20	n.a.	Black mayor
St Louis	20	−0.2	−
Memphis	4	−13.1	−
Average	47	−11.4	

Note
Black representation = Percentage of black councillors on City Council minus black percentage of voting age population.

extent to which blacks have achieved "political incorporation" and the year when this was achieved.

The evidence suggests that the political situation of blacks in each city is indeed linked with the rate of violence. Of the three cities with higher than expected levels, New York and San Francisco were singled out by Browning (1990: 222) as having "weak political incorporation with blacks not in the dominant coalition." The third city, New Orleans, was the only city in Patterson's study in which blacks had *no* political representation on the city council, despite constituting 39.7 percent of the city's voting-age population (1974: 254). Of the eight cities with lower than average rates of violence, five had black mayors. In addition to the political situation, other local factors such as the unemployment rate, police practices, and the activities of the black churches and community leaders, probably play a role in explaining where black terrorism occurred.

Revolutionary leftist terrorism

Support for radical leftist groups was concentrated among students, and a 1970 Gallup survey provides two measures of its extent among this group: the proportion saying they had a highly favorable view of the Weathermen (8 percent) and the proportion identifying themselves as "far left" (7 percent). Taking the larger of these two measures would imply about 604,000 sympathizers.[8] The Weather Underground (as it renamed itself) was a product of the split in the Students for a Democratic Society (SDS) that occurred in 1969. The SDS was founded in 1962, and grew rapidly as the organizational manifestation of the radical anti-Vietnam war movement. At its peak, in November 1968, its membership was estimated at 80,000–100,000 (Sale 1973). Newfield (1966: 118) argues that these figures underestimate the group's true strength, since "for every member, five others take part in SDS activities without paying dues."

The political issues that drove the student radicals were twofold: the struggle for civil rights and opposition to the Vietnam war – especially the latter. Although American involvement in Indo-China began under Truman, and increased significantly under Kennedy, it did not become an issue in American politics until the 1964 election. As the military and political situation deteriorated, President Johnson sent large numbers of troops to Vietnam in an attempt to prevent a communist takeover. This Americanization of the war, beginning in 1965, produced the first real opposition on the campuses and in the media. As the war steadily escalated, so did the dissent. "In its extent and intensity, the

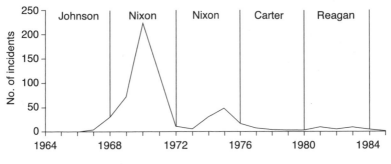

Figure 3.3 Leftist terrorism, 1964–84

antiwar movement in the United States from 1965 through 1971 was the most significant movement of its kind in the nation's history" (Small 1988: 1). Eventually Johnson announced he would not seek a second term, and began to reduce the American involvement in Vietnam. President Nixon, elected with a "secret plan to end the war," initially re-escalated the conflict by bombing and then invading Cambodia. However, he continued to withdraw American forces, and the last US troops left South Vietnam in March 1973.

Puerto Rican separatism

The issue of Puerto Rico's political status dominates Puerto Rican politics, but has a low priority within the United States. The island became by conquest a colony of the United States in 1898. In 1946, the Puerto Rican legislature passed a bill calling for a plebiscite to be held to ascertain the wishes of the people. The appointed American governor vetoed the bill, the legislature overruled his veto, and President Truman, who had the final authority, vetoed the bill on the grounds that approval of the plebiscite "might erroneously be construed by the people of Puerto Rico as a commitment that the United States would accept any plan that might be selected at the proposed plebiscite." However, since the US Congress was unwilling to allow the island either to become independent or to become a state, its ambiguous constitutional status was a potential diplomatic embarrassment in an era of decolonization. Consequently in 1950 Congress passed, and President Truman signed into law on October 30, the Puerto Rican Federal Relations Act, which gave the island a new status as a commonwealth. On the very same day, the Puerto Rican nationalists staged a revolt and declared independence. After the revolt was suppressed, and with virtually the entire nationalist leadership in prison, a referendum was held in 1951 in which Puerto Ricans were given the choice of remaining a colony or approving their new status. Although a large proportion of the electorate abstained, 76 percent of those voting approved commonwealth status.

Since that date, Puerto Rican parties have been divided over the constitutional status issue, with the Popular Democratic Party supporting the current arrangements, and the Statehood Republican Party (later renamed the New Progressive Party) supporting statehood. Two *independista* parties exist, the social democratic Puerto Rican Independence Party (PIP) and the Marxist Puerto Rican Socialist Party. The *independista* vote reached a peak in the 1952 election, with 125,000 votes (19 percent of the total), and then declined. In the two referendums of 1967 and 1993, the independence option received respectively only 0.6 percent and 4.4 percent of the vote. The elections and plebiscites may underestimate the strength of nationalist sentiment, since many *independistas* regard voting as a waste of time, and surveys indicate a somewhat higher percentage preferring the independence option. Surveys also show that a much higher proportion of students are PIP supporters.

Support for terrorism can be gauged by attitudes towards the Macheteros, a terrorist group which has carried out numerous attacks on the island and on the mainland. A 1986 poll conducted by Yankelovich, Skelly, and White revealed that while only 3 percent of the islanders saw the Macheteros as "patriots whose goals justify their means" and 51 percent saw them as "terrorists whose goals and actions are unacceptable," 41 percent thought of them as having "a patriotic cause but that their actions are extreme." The most favorable attitudes were found among *independista* voters, 18 percent of whom were supporters of the Macheteros (cited by Fernandez 1987: 236). If the 3 percent figure is used, then about 65,000 persons on the island were terrorist sympathizers. This does not include sympathizers among the Puerto Rican diaspora on the mainland. Since an equal number of Puerto Ricans live off the island, the total should probably be doubled.[9]

Given the low salience of Puerto Rico as an issue in American politics, it is difficult to classify presidential administrations in terms of their positions on Puerto Rico. However, Puerto Rican terrorist groups often justified their attacks as responses to specific American actions. During his re-election campaign in 1976, President Ford announced his support for Puerto Rican statehood. The issue of Puerto Rico's status was a chronic embarrassment to the United States

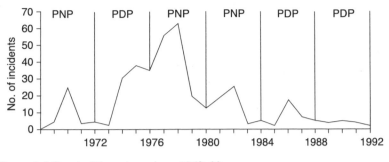

Figure 3.4 Puerto Rican terrorism, 1969–92

at the United Nations, where the Decolonization Committee held hearings and resolutions calling for the island's independence. In 1977, the case of the prisoners who were still in jail for the 1954 shooting in the House of Representatives became an issue, and on September 6, 1979, President Carter released them as an act of executive clemency.

It seems likely that the political situation on Puerto Rico itself would have an effect on the timing of terrorism. According to Nelson (1986: 108), *independistas* saw the statehood movement as a major threat, and if the incidence of terrorism is shown against the periods of rule by the pro-statehood New Progressive Party (PNP), there is an apparent relationship. Terrorism breaks out just after the victory of the PNP in 1969, after twenty-eight years of rule by the Popular Democratic Party (PDP), and peaks during the 1976–80 period when the PNP regained power. When the PDP wins in 1984, terrorism declines to a new low.

The Jewish Defense League and terrorism

The Jewish Defense League (JDL) was formed in 1968 by Meir Kahane. Its social base lay in the cohesive Orthodox Jewish communities of New York City, especially the Crown Heights, Borough Park, and Williamsburg neighborhoods. Feeling threatened by the influx of racial minorities, many welcomed the neighborhood patrols organized by the JDL. "Hundreds of Orthodox Jews, most of them lower middle-class and middle-aged, signed up almost immediately for Kahane's vigilante clubs" (Ziegler 1971: 30). The JDL also organized demonstrations outside Arab embassies, and against the oppression of Soviet Jewry. The latter issue led to an explosion of support among suburban Jews, and a rapid growth of membership. By 1972,

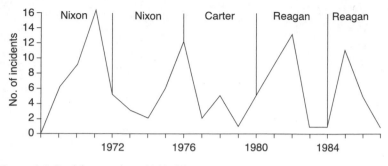

Figure 3.5 Jewish terrorism, 1969–87

the organization claimed 15,000 members. However, most mainstream Jewish organizations were actively hostile to the JDL, and according to the 1984 National Survey of American Jews (Cohen 1984), only 24 percent had a "generally favorable" view of the JDL (while 44 percent had a "generally unfavorable" view and 27 percent had mixed feelings). If those who were generally favorable are considered sympathizers they would number about 864,000. A poll commissioned by the American Jewish Committee found that 14 percent of American Jews "professed strong sympathy for Kahane" (Friedman 1990: 6), which suggests a somewhat lower figure of 504,000 sympathizers.

Cuban *émigré* terrorism

Following the overthrow of Batista and the subsequent Cuban revolution, some 600,000 Cubans emigrated to the United States, the bulk of them settling in Miami. Virtually all the *émigrés* were bitterly hostile to Castro and his regime. In one study of the exiles, all said that only the downfall of the regime would lead them to return to Cuba, 99 percent described Castro as "one of the worst tyrants in the history of Cuba," and 91 percent said that his government contained "no honest and dedicated men" (Fagen *et al.* 1968). Given these sentiments, it is not surprising that many were willing to support violence against Cuba or any supporters of the Cuban government. In 1983 the city of Miami proclaimed March 25 "Orlando Bosch Day," to honor the man who had bombed a Cubana Airlines flight from Venezuela to Havana, killing seventy-three passengers. In the same year, a poll taken by the *Miami Herald* found that 22 percent of Cuban Americans in Dade County believed that anti-Castro terrorism *within* the United

States was justified. The supporters of anti-Castro terrorism therefore presumably numbered about 109,000. Exile organizations proliferated in Miami, and "by 1963 there were so many that the Departments of State and Justice were unable to keep track of them all" (Garcia 1996: 133). A 1968 survey found that 14.4 per cent of the Cubans in their sample were members of an exile political group (Fagen *et al.* 1968: 57), although only a small proportion of the groups engaged in terrorist activities.

After Castro came to power, US–Cuba relations rapidly deteriorated as Cuba aligned itself with the Soviet bloc. In early 1960, Eisenhower approved a CIA plan to recruit and train a Cuban exile army to invade the island and overthrow the Castro regime. Kennedy allowed the invasion to proceed, but the landing at the Bay of Pigs in April 1961 was a disaster, and most of the invaders were killed or captured. Subsequently the Kennedy administration, fearing that Castro would try to export revolution to Latin America, attempted to isolate Cuba diplomatically and economically. The US trade embargo was tightened in February 1962 and, largely as a result of US pressure, the Organization of American States voted to limit Cuban participation in its activities, and embargoed arms shipments to Cuba. Fourteen Latin American nations were persuaded to break off diplomatic relations. In addition to these overt acts, the Kennedy administration plotted to assassinate Castro, and the CIA continued its sponsorship of raids and sabotage by exile groups. Garcia (1996: 127–9) comments that "the exile community was a wild card, testing, threatening, and sometimes even dictating policy. The CIA found it difficult to control the groups on its payroll: raids cancelled by CIA personnel in Miami were frequently carried out anyway by the impatient *émigrés*. . . . It became difficult to distinguish raids sanctioned by the CIA from those that were not." After the Cuban missile crisis of October 1962, the Kennedy administration was afraid of being drawn into a full-scale war with the Soviet Union, and on March 30, 1963, announced a crackdown on raids by exile groups. In fact, although many raiding parties were intercepted, only a few individuals were prosecuted and given token fines. After Kennedy's death, Johnson[10] essentially maintained his policy of hostility to the Cuban regime, including the economic embargo. Under Nixon and Ford, relations with Cuba were improved as part of a general policy of *détente* with the Soviet bloc. An anti-hijacking treaty was signed in 1973, and in 1975 the United States voted in favor of the OAS lifting its trade embargo of the island. However, relations again worsened after Castro sent

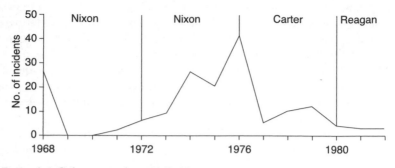

Figure 3.6 Cuban terrorism, 1968–82

troops to the Congo and Angola in the late 1970s. Under the Carter administration a further normalization of relations took place (Paterson 1994; Garcia 1996).

If Cuban *émigré* violence *within* the United States is examined in relation to US government policy, an obvious relationship can be seen. When the government was not only sympathetic but actively encouraging *la causa* – the attempt to overthrow Castro – there was no domestic terrorism. When the American government abandoned this policy, and began to normalize relations with Cuba, "many *émigrés* were enraged. . . . Angered by the new developments in American foreign policy and what they perceived to be a growing complacency in the exile community, the militant extremists escalated the war against Cuba" (Garcia 1996: 138, 140).

Anti-abortion terrorism

Public opinion on abortion is clearly ambivalent, and the answers are very obviously affected by how the question is worded.[11] The number who feel strongly about the issue can be calculated from a 1989 poll, which found that 32 percent favored overturning the Roe decision (compared with 62 percent who supported it), but that the anti-Roe group had more intense opinions. Since 41 percent of those who were anti-Roe had "extremely strong" opinions on the issue, this means that 13 percent of the general American population were strongly anti-abortion (compared with 10 percent who were strongly pro-choice). As numerous studies have shown, the primary factor predicting attitudes towards abortion is religion, with fundamentalist Protestants and devout Catholics being the most opposed to abortion. This is the case not only among the general population, but also among

activists (Luker 1984; Granberg 1981). Obviously, only a small proportion of those who are strongly opposed to abortion are willing to use
violence or even to engage in any type of political action. There are
no national polls that measure the degree of sympathy for extremist
anti-abortion groups. However, a survey by Guth (1994) of a sample
of eight conservative Protestant organizations with a membership of
approximately 1 million found that 14.4 percent felt "very close" to
Operation Rescue, which advocates passive resistance against abortion
clinics. This suggests about 144,000 conservative Protestant sympathizers and, since Scott and Schuman (1988) found an equal number
of Catholics and fundamentalists were strongly opposed to abortion,
implies that the national total might be about 300,000. The number
who attend the annual March for Life is used as an indicator of anti-
abortion mobilization. The marchers have numbered between 50,000
and 70,000, with no obvious trend since the 1970s. Operation Rescue
claimed to have over 35,000 members in 200 cities, and thousands of
demonstrators have been arrested for blockading clinics.

Blanchard and Prewitt (1993) in their study of anti-abortion violence
suggest two ways in which the political context affected the level of
violence. First, they argue that there was more violence under
Reagan than under Carter because of his administration's position
on abortion. For example, Attorney General Meese filed a "friend of
the court" brief with the Supreme Court in July 1985, supporting the
reversal of Roe *v.* Wade, and in October of the same year Reagan
proposed that Congress deny funding to family planning clinics that
provided abortion information – the so-called gag rule. "Whatever
the chief executive's actual intentions, the administration's stance on
the issue was perceived by some extremists as endorsement and legiti-
mization of private law enforcement or vigilantism" (1993: 271).

Second, they argue that Reagan's speeches and writings themselves
had an effect. "The wide circulation of [an anti-abortion] essay . . .
was followed by a drastic increase in the rate of abortion-related
violence, and the president's speeches before anti-abortion groups
were interpreted by the violent radicals as tacit approval." Indeed,
his failure to speak out against clinic bombings was also a factor.
"While we cannot prove a direct cause-and-effect relationship between
Reagan's silence and abortion-related violence, the correlation is evi
dent in the decline in violence following his eventual public condem-
nation of it" (1993: 270).

The argument that "Reagan's stance on the abortion issue could
only have encouraged the increase in violence" implicitly exaggerates
the differences between Reagan and Carter's policies. Carter repeatedly

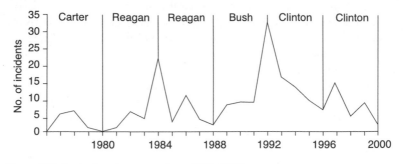

Figure 3.7 Anti-abortion terrorism, 1977–2000

stated that he was opposed to federal funding of abortion, and in one televised interview said that "any abortion is too much." The National Organization of Women opposed his candidacy in 1980, because of his lack of commitment to abortion rights. During the Carter presidency, the House of Representatives several times approved restrictions on federal funding of abortions, and also voted in favor of a ban on abortions being performed on military bases using defense funds. Surely, if we accept Blanchard and Prewitt's argument, these actions should also have legitimated anti-abortion violence?

The Bush administration continued Reagan's policies on the abortion issue. Bush called for Roe to be overturned, and twice vetoed legislation that would have lifted the gag rule. The Justice Department joined with Operation Rescue in an appeal to stay a preliminary injunction banning pickets from blocking access to abortion clinics. Like Reagan, President Bush and Vice-president Quayle spoke to the National Right to Life Conventions. Yet despite the marked similarities between the two administrations, abortion violence declined in Reagan's second term but increased under Bush.

Clinton's campaign rhetoric was strongly pro-choice, and one of his first acts was to lift abortion restrictions imposed under Reagan and Bush. Abortion became an option in federal employee health plans, and states were required to pay for Medicaid abortions. Under Clinton, picketing outside abortion clinics was severely restricted by the Freedom of Access to Clinics Entrance Law. The Justice Department launched an aggressive probe of the anti-abortion movement in a futile attempt to discover a national conspiracy of violence against the clinics. Clinton's pro-choice stance was so uncompromising that he vetoed a bill calling for the end of partial-birth abortions. Surely, if Blanchard and Prewitt's logic is correct, this should have resulted in a decline in the number of anti-abortion incidents? In fact, not only did the level of violence remain the same, but the attacks became more deadly. All the murders by anti-abortionists took place during the Clinton presidency.

Far right terrorism

The degree of support for contemporary right-wing extremism is difficult to estimate, in large part because there is no agreed-upon definition of "right-wing extremism." The movement is multifaceted, and hence the political space it occupies is unclear. Writers see different elements as significant, variously labeling the movement and its adherents as white racists, white supremacists, the patriot movement, the militia, etc. Hamm (1993: 50) emphasizes the movement's eclectic diversity, describing it as a "secret collective of paramilitary survivalists, tax protesters, bankrupt farmers, bikers, prisoners, Odinists and devotees of the Identity Church, linked together by an elaborate network of computer boards, desktop publications and telephone hotlines." Dees (1996: 10) provides an even more expansive definition of "the Patriot movement," and sees it as including "on its moderate side the John Birch society and the conspiratorial segment of televangelist Pat Robertson's audience [while] on the movement's more militant side are groups like the American Christian Patriots, Posse Comitatus, and Christian Identity." Dees believes the movement has "about five million followers."

This may seem a high figure, yet polls show that many of the key ideological beliefs of the violent right – such as hostility to the federal government or a belief in Jewish power – are accepted by a remarkable number of Americans. According to Gallup polls taken shortly after the Oklahoma City bombing, 18 percent of Americans believe that ordinary citizens should be "allowed to arm and organize themselves in order to resist the powers of the federal government," 8 percent see the federal government as an "enemy," and 5 percent would "personally support an armed citizen rebellion or uprising" (*Gallup Poll Monthly* May, October 1995). If the 5 percent figure is used as the basis for estimating the number of sympathizers, Dees's figure of 5 million would seem to be on the low side.

Although few Americans believe that they live under a "Zionist occupational government," polls show that a significant minority think "Jews have too much power," with the number almost doubling from 13 percent in 1964 to 23 percent in 1981 (Martire 1982).[12] In areas such as the farm belt, antisemitism is widespread, and a 1986 Harris survey found 43 percent of Iowa and Nebraska residents held strongly antisemitic views (Coates 1987: 197).

The number of right-wing sympathizers who are mobilized, in some sense or another, is equally uncertain. The most widely cited estimate is that, by the late 1990s, white supremacist groups had between 100,000 and 200,000 members, the total including "active sympathizers who buy literature, make contributions, and attend periodic meetings" (Dobratz and Shanks-Meile 1997: 25). Estimates as to the number in each subcategory vary widely. For example, estimates of the number of Christian Identity adherents range "from two thousand to over fifty thousand" (Barkun 1994: viii). Similarly, Coates (1987: 111) claims that there may have been over 57,000 members of Posse Comitatus in the early 1980s, while George and Wilcox (1992: 346) suggest the group "never had more than one thousand *bona fide* members at any given time." The militia movement has been credited with "15,000 members" (by the Anti-defamation League), "20,000 active volunteers" (by *The Nation*), "10,000 to 40,000 members" (by *The Progressive*), "a total of 30,000 to 40,000 members" (by the Southern Poverty Law Center), and "up to 50,000 members" (by *USA Today*). Again George and Wilcox (1992: 255–8) are skeptical, suggesting that the real figure was "probably under 5,000." It should be noted that the high figures come from liberal watchdog organizations such as the Southern Poverty Law Center and Political Research Associates, that are motivated to exaggerate the danger of these groups to attract funds. However, the lower estimate of 100,000 as a total is not unreasonable, and is used here.[13]

What of the political context in which right-wing terrorism emerged? As noted earlier, many liberals blamed the conservative climate of the Reagan years, but not all who have studied the movement agree. According to Singular (1987: 85), "Instead of welcoming the conservative shift in the country [the extremists] tended to loathe it, for it drew members from their ranks towards more conventional center-right politics. It left them isolated on the fringe." Hamm (1993: 50) argues that "the American neo-Nazis began with an aggressive rejection of the symbols of eighties conservatism." It should also be pointed out that mainstream conservatives reciprocated their hostility, and that Edwin Meese, Reagan's Attorney General, launched an aggressive – though unsuccessful – prosecution of the movement's leaders. From an Aryan/white separatist perspective, Reagan was certainly no friend, and his social circle and administration contained a significant number of Jews. Both the Reagan/Bush and the Clinton administrations would

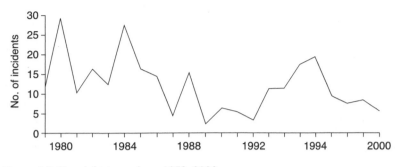

Figure 3.8 Far right terrorism, 1979–2000

appear equally unsympathetic, and one would anticipate little difference in the level of violence between the two periods. During the
Reagan/Bush years (1981–92) the total number of incidents was 130,
or an annual average of 10.8, while during the Clinton years the total
was eighty-two, or an annual average of 11.7. The terrorism during
the Clinton years was, however, significantly more deadly in terms of
the number killed and wounded.[14]

Islamic fundamentalist terrorism

The hostility of many Muslims towards the United States is often
attributed to their distaste for its modern, secular, plural values and
way of life. A variant of this theory argues that hatred of the West
results from the failure of Arab societies to modernize successfully.
Autocratic and inefficient Arab regimes encourage anti-American
and anti-Israeli sentiments as a way of displacing popular resentment.
    If we consider what the terrorists themselves say, it appears that US
foreign policy, especially American support for Israel, is what moti-
vates their actions. In 1993, when the World Trade Center was
bombed by Islamic fundamentalists, the writer of a *Newsweek* article,
entitled "A terrorist plot without a story," pronounced himself puzzled
by the lack of "a coherent reason for bombing the World Trade
Center . . . the best we have are vague references to US support for
Israel" (Morgenthau 1994). Of course, to most Arabs and Muslims
US support for Israel is such a glaring injustice that a vague reference
is all that is necessary. Articles on the radical Islamic movement emphasize its intense hostility to Israel and to Jews (Adams 1993: 78; Bernstein 1994; Chesnoff 1993: 35; Emerson 1995: 42, 48). One militant is

quoted by Emerson as saying, "the Islamic Jihad movement sees Israel and America as two faces of the same coin." Osama bin Laden himself explained his grievances against America in a *fatwa* issued in February 1998. The United States was occupying Saudi Arabia and its holy places (Mecca and Medina), was enforcing sanctions against Iraq, and was supporting Israel in its oppression of the Palestinian people. When the American attacks on Afghanistan began, he implicitly acknowledged his role in the World Trade Center attack, and declared that Americans would not be secure in their land as long as the Palestinians were not secure in theirs.

The growing strength of Islamic fundamentalism has inspired attacks on American targets throughout the world. However, the ability of Islamic radicals to strike at *domestic* American targets is dependent upon two factors, poor immigration control at US frontiers and the growth of an Islamic community within the United States. A combination of immigration and conversion resulted by the late 1990s in a Muslim population estimated at between 2 million and 6 million, of whom about a third are Arabs, and a third American-born converts (mainly blacks). Iranians and Pakistanis make up most of the remainder.[15]

Even those most concerned about the dangers of Islamic terrorism within America acknowledge that only a small minority of American Muslims support terrorism. Adams (1993: 77) talks of how "Nearly all [Muslim immigrants] reject Teheran's calls for terrorist violence. But a growing minority are being influenced by revolutionary organizers." Steven Emerson (1995: 39), producer of the PBS documentary *Jihad in America*, notes that "the vast majority of Muslims in America are peaceful and law-abiding and do not condone violence. But in recent years an extremist fringe of militant Islam has taken root here." If nothing else, the existence of a sizable Muslim community allows potential terrorists to blend in without attracting attention.

Some estimates are available as to the number who belong to radical Islamic groups. An article in *US News & World Report* (Chesnoff 1993: 35) claims that "the number and diversity of radical Islamic and Palestinian organizations operating here is dizzying," and that some are linked with active terrorist groups such as Islamic Jihad and Hezbollah. Adams (1993) suggests that the most important organizations are HAMAS ("4,000 supporters and sympathizers") and Hezbollah ("Its US membership now approaches several thousand.") Emerson (1995: 41) notes that the 1994 convention of the Muslim Arab Youth Association (linked with the Muslim Brotherhood) was attended by 5,000 people. Al-Fuqra is estimated to have 3,000 US followers, most of

them African-American converts. Allowing for some smaller group,
a total of 20,000 seems reasonable.

Discussion

Based on the American experience prior to the September 11 attack,
some generalizations can be made as to the political background to
terrorism. First, sustained outbreaks of terrorism are associated with
the existence of a substantial body of sympathizers and supporters.
In every one of the cases examined, a sizable number of people felt
very strongly about some social/political issue, and also felt that the
political system ignored, or was hostile to, their concerns. The timing
of each outbreak of terrorism coincides, at least approximately, with
the rise of extremist sentiments and with various indicators of extremist
mobilization.

In Table 3.4 the terrorist campaigns are first ranked in terms of
severity (i.e. how many terrorist incidents and how many terrorist-
caused deaths). Then in the second column (headed "Sympathizers")
the estimated number of those who support violent extremist groups
is given. In the third column (headed "Mobilized") are shown the numbers of those who are linked with extremist organizations of varying
degrees of militancy.

Since we have two kinds of measures of extremism, we can ask which
is more closely linked with the amount of violence – the number of
extremist sympathizers or the number who are mobilized? Eudora
Welty in an article about the murder of the civil rights leader, Medger
Evers, claimed that "even if she did not know the killer's name, she

Table 3.4 Number of terrorist incidents/deaths, extremist sympathizers and
mobilized supporters, by ideological category

Ideological category	Incidents (deaths)	Sympathizers	Mobilized
Klan/segregationists	588 (65)	1,660,000	305,000
Revolutionaries	684 (13)	604,000	100,000
Black militants	475 (165)	2,000,000	255,000
Rightists	252 (110)	5,000,000	100,000
Puerto Ricans	383 (29)	130,000	92,000
Anti-abortionists	202 (6)	300,000	75,000
Anti-Castro Cubans	112 (10)	109,000	71,000
Jewish militants	115 (5)	504,000	15,000
Islamic militants	35 (11)	?	20,000

knew him just the same. He could have been almost any white segregationist in Mississippi." An FBI agent assigned to the case made a similar point. "Even if Byron de la Beckwith had not murdered him, he would have been murdered in any case, by someone else" (Massengill 1994: 142, 153). This suggests that the more pro-violent extremists there are the more violence there will be.

However, terrorism is not usually carried out by lone individuals, acting in isolation. To the extent that individuals holding extremist views come into contact with other like-minded individuals, their militancy is likely to be reinforced. An account of the events leading up to the Ruby Ridge incident (Bock 1995: 40) describes how Randy and Vicki Weaver became more extremist. "Slowly as they talked to other people in similar circumstances to them, they began to accept more white separatist ideas." Contact between extremists is most likely to occur when they are mobilized by organizations. Extremist organizations attract individuals with extreme opinions, and disseminate extreme ideologies. Therefore members of such organizations are likely to have their views reinforced, and to feel that violence is legitimate and encouraged. This has been noted for both left-wing and right-wing movements. Members of the Students for a Democratic Society and the anti-war movement "found themselves in the midst of hundreds of anti-war marchers. In addition to the exhilaration of that kind of experience, black, student, and SDS leaders and troops were convinced by media attention . . . that they were part of a great movement very near to success" (Conlin 1982: 219). Dees (1996: 200) argues that "although most militia members may be law-abiding citizens, militia groups attract those with a propensity for violence and act as a springboard for their activities. . . . They bring together like-minded people who may embolden one another and go on to form their own secret cell."

To see which is the more important factor, the data of Table 3.4 are presented in graphic form in Figures 3.9, 3.10, and 3.11. Figure 3.9 shows the relationship between the number of sympathizers and the number of terrorist incidents, while Figure 3.10 shows the relationship between the number mobilized and the number of terrorist incidents. It appears that mobilization is more important, since there is a close relationship between the mobilization measures and the amount of violence, while the number of extremist sympathizers seems unrelated to the amount of violence. In Figure 3.11 the terrorist incidents are weighted according to severity (by adding the terrorist fatalities to the number of incidents), and an even stronger relationship between mobilization and the amount of violence is apparent. It is noticeable

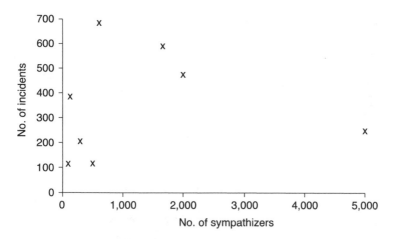

Figure 3.9 Sympathizers and incidents

that, in all three figures, the amount of revolutionary leftist violence is greater than would be expected on the basis of the number of sympathizers and their degree of mobilization.[16]

A second generalization that can be made concerns the effect of the political climate upon the incidence of terrorism. The claim that sympathetic administrations encourage terrorism is clearly false. If presidential administrations are categorized according to their positions on racial segregation, racial equality, the Vietnam war, Cuba, and

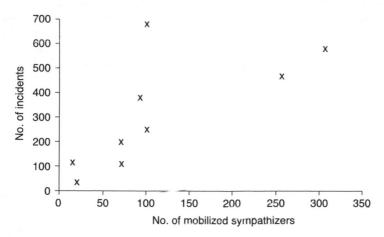

Figure 3.10 Mobilized sympathizers and incidents

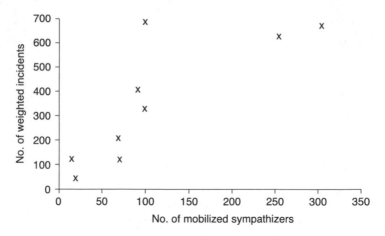

Figure 3.11 Mobilized sympathizers and weighted incidents

abortion, the level of terrorist violence, in almost all cases, is higher under *unsympathetic* administrations than under sympathetic administrations. In the case of Puerto Rican terrorism, terrorist activity was higher under the pro-statehood PNP than under PDP governors. According to my calculations – which are based on the preceding descriptions of the political climate – in seventeen instances high levels of terrorism occurred under unsympathetic administrations, while there were nine cases in which sympathetic administrations experienced relatively low levels of terrorism. In only three cases did terrorism increase or remain at a high level under sympathetic administrations, and in only one case was there little or no terrorism under an unsympathetic administration. There is obviously a certain subjective element in defining what is a "sympathetic" administration, and also in deciding what is a "high" compared with a "low" level of terrorism, but the overall pattern is clear.[17]

As Davies (1971) noted in his classic study *When Men Revolt and Why*, the resort to violence is most likely to take place when members of a group have their hopes and aspirations raised, but then become disillusioned with the political process. In several of the cases examined, this effect can be observed. Reagan raised the expectations of the religious right in general, and anti-abortion activists in particular. Yet, as the columnist E. J. Dionne pointed out, "It is striking how much loyalty Ronald Reagan won from this constituency without delivering much to them at all. . . . There was no school prayer amend ment, no anti-abortion amendment, no school choice program. Most of their core issues were just not dealt with" (cited in Martin 1996). Eventually, frustration at the lack of results from peaceful political activity led a few individuals to turn to violence.

A similar pattern can be discerned in the anti-Vietnam war movement, and the violence carried out by the Weather Underground and other radical groups. The opposition to the war took a variety of forms ranging "from petitions and rallies and teach-ins and electoral campaigns, to public fasting, draft resistance, and even, towards the end, rudimentary forms of insurrection" (Powers 1973: xiii). Two things should be noted about the violence: that it was carried out by a small minority, and that it occurred *after* 1968. Those who participated in the anti-war movement initially perceived themselves to be successful in changing both public opinion and American policy. Activists saw their efforts culminating in Johnson's announcement of March 1968 that he would not run for the presidency. Small (1988: 158) describes how "immediately following the completion of his speech, students poured out of dormitories all across the nation in spontaneous demonstrations, congratulating themselves." One journalist concluded that the speech was a "stunning victory" for the anti-war movement (Schell 1976: 18). However, this apparent victory was followed by the election of Nixon and the continuation of the war. This led to the "widespread belief [among activists] that the opposition to the war had failed completely, that Johnson's defeat in 1968 had been meaningless and empty, that Nixon was simply pursuing the war with equal determination by other means" (Powers 1973: xix). The turn to violence on the part of the Weathermen grew "out of a sense of rage and deep frustration . . . at the continuing war in Vietnam" (Zaroulis and Sullivan 1984: 314).

The resort to violence by black militants also fits this pattern. Civil rights initiatives under Eisenhower, Kennedy, and Johnson raised black aspirations, but the pace of reforms fell short of what many blacks wanted, and their frustration led to both widespread rioting and the emergence of violence-prone black nationalist and separatist groups. With the election of Nixon and white backlash, the gap between black demands and government policy became so great that it led to widespread violence.

Cuban *émigré* violence is also linked with raised hopes followed by frustration. Initially the US government not only encouraged exile hopes of overthrowing Castro, but armed and trained them for this purpose. When American policy changed, many exiles felt enraged by what they saw as a betrayal. The increasing violence in 1976–78 was "a result of the Carter administration's new policies towards Cuba." One militant noted that "It is to be expected that after eighteen years in exile a frustrated generation would emerge whose impatience would lead them to use extreme methods" (Garcia 1996: 140–1). Under the Reagan administration, which set up Radio Marti and took a generally hard line against the Castro regime (which was accused of backing the insurgents in El Salvador), the level of violence went down again.

In the case of segregationist violence, we need a different explanation for the interplay between politics and violence. Segregationist violence was essentially reactive to both challenges by the civil rights movement and federal intervention on behalf of southern blacks, and the timing of the violence reflects this. The fact that Klan activity declines in the late 1960s is usually attributed to vigorous law enforcement by the FBI. Wade (1987: 364) points out that another

> factor in the Klan's deterioration in the late 1960s has received little attention: the Presidential campaigns of George C. Wallace. . . . It's now clear that Wallace's campaigns as the American Independent Party candidate swallowed a lot of disaffected Klansmen. In fact Wallace offered them the first really viable alternative to the Klan. . . . The Wallace campaigns successfully skimmed the Southern Klans of their most effective and economically well-off supporters. There was hardly anything left of the Southern Klan but leaderless dregs.

Following the 1968 election, Nixon's "southern strategy" – essentially an attempt to coopt Wallace voters – further weakened the Klan by providing a political alternative to those who felt threatened by the changes in race relations.

The evidence suggests that terrorism is used by those who can see little chance of getting what they want through regular political channels. They turn to bullets because ballots do not work. Since politics is, in some respects, a zero-sum game in which one group's gain is another's loss, even the most open and responsive democracy cannot satisfy all groups consistently. For example, black demands for civil rights were incompatible with the maintenance of segregation. Groups that lose in the political game – particularly if they lose consistently – are likely to find the resort to violence a tempting option.

Notes

1 The FBI's estimate of 40,000 for 1965 is close to that of the Anti-defamation League, but the House Committee on Un-American Activities report gives a much lower figure of 16,800 for 1967.
2 Although Kennedy had pledged during his 1960 election campaign to ban racial discrimination in federally assisted housing, he delayed issuing the order until November 1962.
3 Using the southern governors' speeches reported in Sarratt as an indicator, the number of segregationist and extremist speeches, by state, was Arkansas (twelve), Mississippi (eleven), Virginia (ten), Alabama (seven), Louisiana (four), Georgia (four), Florida (two), South Carolina (one), and North Carolina (one).
4 In the 1960 presidential elections, the National States' Rights Party was on the ballot in four southern states, while "unpledged Democrats" won all of Mississippi's electoral votes and six out of Alabama's eleven electoral votes. The 1964 Goldwater vote and the 1968 Wallace vote are considered segregationist.
5 Editors who deviated from the segregationist position lost readers and advertising. Some were driven out of business, assaulted on the street, or had their offices bombed. Hodding Carter of the *Delta Democrat-Times* was hanged in effigy (Sarratt 1966: 256–8).
6 Both the Panthers and the black Muslims were largely drawn from the urban underclass, and both had a significant criminal element (Anthony 1990: 102; Friedly 1992: 176).
7 Essien-Udom distinguishes between different degrees of involvement, and estimated that in 1960 there were "between 5,000 and 15,000 registered followers, at least 50,000 believers, and a much larger number of sympathizers" (1962: 71). Clegg (1997: 115) suggests 20,000 members as the high point in the early 1960s, with "tens of thousands" of sympathizers.
8 The two measures are not as correlated as one might assume, and some who had a favorable view of the Weathermen identified themselves as "far right" politically.
9 This presumes that attitudes were similar on Puerto Rico and the mainland. Given the high degree of back-and-forth migration, and the fact that many *independistas* convicted of terrorism had been brought up on the mainland, this seems a reasonable assumption.
10 "What can I do that won't get me in trouble?" Johnson asked McGeorge Bundy, but soon decided that he had little option but to maintain a hostile stance (Paterson 1994: 262).
11 In one 1980 poll, when respondents were first asked if they supported a constitutional ban on abortions, 62 percent were opposed and 29 percent in favor, but when asked later about their opinion on a constitutional amendment "protecting the life of the unborn child," they supported the amendment 50 percent to 39 percent (Craig 1993: 264–71).
12 I have been unable to find more recent surveys on this particular question. In a poll released by the Anti-defamation League on its web site www.adl.org 25 percent of those surveyed thought that "Jews are more loyal to Israel than America." In 1998 the figure was 31 percent.

13 It is interesting that over 200,000 copies of *The Turner Diaries* have been sold since 1978 – a figure very similar to that of the high estimate of the membership of white supremacist groups. While some copies are in the hands of academic researchers and law enforcement officials, I suspect that most are purchased by those who agree with the book's sentiments.

14 Thus eighty deaths and injuries resulted from terrorist attacks during 1981–92 and 194 deaths and injuries (not including the Oklahoma City casualties) during 1993–99, an annual average four times as great.

15 The high figure comes from the Council on American–Islamic Relations, the low figure from a study commissioned by the American Jewish Committee (Broadway 2001).

16 This could be partially explained by the demographics of the revolutionary leftists. The Students for a Democratic Society were young and hence more likely to act upon their extremist beliefs. Also since they were committed to gender equality, leftists had a larger pool of potential recruits and many revolutionary leftist terrorists were women.

17 All presidential administrations were considered unsympathetic to the far right. Jewish terrorism is ignored, since it was linked with local issues such as street crime rather than federal policy.

4 The organizational dynamics of terrorism

The previous chapter showed two things: first that terrorism usually occurred when the political system was unresponsive or hostile to the concerns of certain groups, and second that each and every wave of terrorism was associated with the existence of a body of sympathizers and supporters. The closest association appeared to be between organizational mobilization (i.e. the number who participate in some extremist movement) and terrorist violence. In the first section of this chapter, the relationship between terrorist violence and the organizational growth and decline of extremist movements will be examined in more detail.

Social movements and the emergence of terrorism

In several instances, the emergence of terrorist groups and terrorist violence is linked historically with the decline of social movements, this decline often coinciding with the splitting of the movement into competing ideological factions. In the south, the membership of the non-violent and respectable White Citizens' Councils reached a peak in 1957, and then tumbled to 23,000 in 1963 (McMillen 1971: 153–4), before Klan violence and membership surged. Nelson (1993: 39) suggests a link between the two phenomena, at least for Mississippi, pointing out that "the councils were so effective that . . . the Klan did not become a major factor in Mississippi until Sam Bowers organized the White Knights in 1964."

In the case of the anti-war movement, a similar pattern is observable. The Students for a Democratic Society (SDS) grew rapidly from 1964 until 1968, then split into hostile ideological factions at its 1969 convention, and its membership plummeted. Revolutionary terrorism was both cause and consequence of this split, since one of the three factions

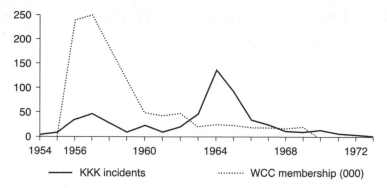

Figure 4.1 The decline of the White Citizens' Councils and Klan terrorism, 1954–73

became the Weathermen, who argued that armed struggle (i.e. terrorism) would bring about a revolutionary situation.

The history of both the Black Panthers and the Black Muslims also shows a clear link between organizational splits and violence. The Muslims grew steadily in the 1950s, from a few hundred at the beginning of the decade to thousands in 1959, and this was followed by an upsurge in the early 1960s after they received increased media coverage. However, when Malcolm X broke away in 1964 and set up the Organization of African Unity, there were large-scale defections from the Nation of Islam, and violence flared up between his followers and those who remained loyal to Elijah Muhammad. The Nation was

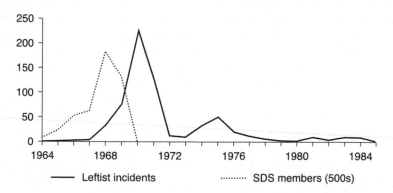

Figure 4.2 The decline of the Students for a Democratic Society and leftist terrorism, 1964–85

racked by another round of internal dissension in the early 1970s, which led to further bloodshed.

> The conflict was related to Muhammad's age and incessant health problems, as some Muslims perhaps desired to gain advantage before a war over succession broke out. Also the internecine struggles were related to resurgent ideological issues that pitted idealistic young Turks against the conservative, acquisitive Old Guard. . . . Factions operating in New York, Oakland and Baton Rouge seemed to be loosely connected at best; some claimed to still revere Elijah Muhammad as their spiritual leader while others seceded from the Nation altogether.
>
> (Clegg 1997: 260–1)

The Black Panther Party, founded in 1966, grew rapidly until dissension between Eldridge Cleaver and Huey Newton led to the emergence of two organizations in early 1971, with several deaths resulting from the rivalry between them. The Black Liberation Army, which split off from the Black Panthers at this time, was the militant wing of the Eldridge Cleaver faction (Daley 1973). While the Panthers advocated "self-defense" against the police, the BLA adopted a policy of deliberately gunning them down.

In the Puerto Rican case, the strength of the *independista* movement can be gauged from election results. In the immediate post-war period, independence sentiments were widespread. The Popular Democratic Party won a decisive victory in the 1944 elections, taking 66 percent of the vote, and most of those elected were *independistas* (Fernandez 1994: 57). When Munoz Marin, the leader of the PDP, backed commonwealth status for the island rather than independence, the

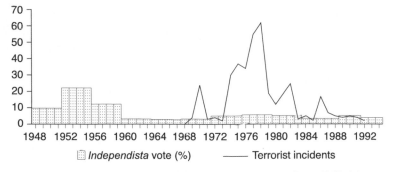

Figure 4.3 The *independista* vote and Puerto Rican terrorism, 1948–94

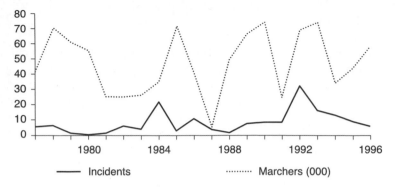

Figure 4.4 Anti-abortion terrorism and the March for Life turnout, 1977–96

independista wing split off and formed the Puerto Rican Independence Party (PIP). PIP received 10.4 percent of the vote in 1948, 19.0 percent in 1952, and 12.5 percent in 1956. The sharp decline in the *independista* vote in the 1960 elections is followed, a few years later, by a wave of terrorism beginning in the late 1960s.[1]

Attacks on abortion clinics, however, do not appear to be linked with the decline of the anti-abortion movement or to splits within it. The mobilization of the anti-abortion movement is indicated by the turnout for the annual March for Life rallies. Starting in 1974, the turnout, as estimated by the Park Police and reported in the *Washington Post*, first increases, drops during Reagan's first term, and then rebounds, with no obvious correlation between the turnout for the marches and the number of attacks.[2]

Whether the far right was in decline when terrorism broke out in 1979 is difficult to determine and depends upon what measures are used. Hamm (1993: 49) argues that it was.

> By mid-decade the membership in the Ku Klux Klan had fallen from a high of 11,500 in 1981 to about 5,000 in 1985, and membership in the American Nazi Party dwindled from 1,200 to about 400 during the same period. Large Klan rallies began tapering off; Klan and neo-Nazi leaders started fighting with each other, and eventually more than thirty different Klan and neo-Nazi organizations emerged.

However, another indicator of racial-nationalist mobilization, the vote for the Populist Party, shows a resurgence during the 1980s and early 1990s. Diamond (1995: 262–3) sees the Populist Party's 1984 presidential campaign as "the racist Right's first concerted foray into electoral politics" since George Wallace's 1968 campaign. The party was organized by veterans of the racist right and its national chairman was a former Klan leader. Although on the ballot in only fourteen states, the party won 66,000 votes in 1984. With David Duke as their candidate the vote declined to 47,000 in 1988, but then increased to 107,000 when Bo Gritz ran in 1992.

The organization of terrorism

Some writers such as Trick (NACCJSG 1976) define terrorism so that it includes only acts committed by organized groups. Similarly the FBI is reluctant to categorize an incident as terrorism unless it is claimed by a group. In this study, terrorism is defined more broadly as any deliberate act of violence carried out for political or social reasons. However, in order to understand terrorism (and to take appropriate countermeasures) it is useful to distinguish between organized and unorganized terrorism.

Most terrorism is organized in the sense that it is carried out by members of terrorist or extremist organizations. It is difficult to be sure exactly what proportion, since many attacks are unclaimed,[3] but if we consider those who are arrested for terrorist offences, we find that 91 percent are members of, or in some way connected with, such organizations. The remainder are lone individuals (2 percent), or informal groups of friends (7 percent). Even those individuals who are not members of organized groups may have links with wider movements, and respond to what the leaders of extremist movements do and say. This question will be examined in the next chapter, which looks at the characteristics of individuals who engage in terrorist acts, and their terrorist careers. The extent to which the different ideological categories of terrorism are organized varies significantly, as Table 4.1 shows.

It should be noted, however, that even the most "organized" categories are far from monolithic, with a multiplicity of extremist organization and terrorist groups whose members engaged in violence. My data set records eighty-one named extremist or terrorist groups, of which forty-two were right-wing (seventeen in the first wave, twenty-five in the second), and eighteen left-wing, as well as seventeen black groups, ten Cuban groups, six Puerto Rican groups, and four Jewish groups. The American situation is, in this respect, very different from that found in Northern Ireland, the Basque region of Spain, Italy,

Table 4.1 Affiliation of those committing terrorist offences

Ideology	Extremist organizations	Terrorist groups	Unaffiliated
Segregationist	88.8		11.2
Black	78.3	17.3	4.4
Leftist		84.3	15.7
Puerto Rican		100.0	
Jewish	100.0		
Cuban		100.0	
Anti-abortionist			100.0
Rightist	48.6	22.7	28.7

and West Germany, where one or two groups are responsible for most of the violence.

Most of the terrorism in the south during the civil rights period was carried out by Klan members, and similarly most black militants who engaged in violence were members of the Black Panther Party or the Nation of Islam. Puerto Rican terrorism was carried out by organized terrorist groups, mainly by the FALN and the Macheteros, while Jewish terrorism involved members of the Jewish Defense League or one of its splinter groups. At the other extreme are the contemporary anti-abortionist and far right terrorists. All the three anti-abortionist killers (John Salvi, Paul Hill, and Michael Griffin) seem to have been loners, operating on the fringes of the Pro-life movement. Those convicted of arson or bombing attacks against abortion clinics were either individuals or informal groups of friends. Although the "Army of God" name was used on several occasions by various individuals or informal groups, it appears to have been a rhetorical device, not an indication of organizational links.

The contemporary far right appears to have adopted the strategy of "leaderless resistance" advocated by Louis Beam, with lone individuals responsible for a large number of attacks. Among them are four serial racist killers: John Paul Franklin, Joseph Christopher, Frank Spisak, and Neal Long. More recently, we have the cases of Timothy McVeigh, the Oklahoma City bomber, Eric Rudolph, who bombed the Olympic park in Atlanta, and Buford Furrow, who went on a shooting rampage against a Jewish community center.[4]

Although not so amorphous, both Cuban and revolutionary terrorism were organized in an extremely fluid fashion. *Emigré* Cuban terrorist organizations "frequently disbanded, and their members created new splinter groups giving the impression that there were more terrorists than there actually were." According to one police investigator: "I can say that we have more than ten militant groups with hard core militants . . . those ten groups may be twelve tomorrow and next week there may be fifty, and then the week after it may be down to eight" (Garcia 1996: 147). Revolutionary terrorist groups had a similarly loose structure; individuals frequently moved between organizations (Klehr 1986: 109), and joint actions and coalitions were common. For example, the M19 Communist Organization (M19CO), which carried out a robbery of a Brinks truck in October 1981, was an alliance between the remnants of the Weather Underground and the Black Liberation Army (Castellucci 1986: 133).[5]

Terrorism by members of extremist organizations

In analyzing how terrorism is organized, it is useful to distinguish between two types of entities: extremist above-ground organizations and terrorist groups. The former engage in legitimate political or religious activities, while the sole purpose of the latter is terrorism. As examples of mass organizations we have the Nation of Islam, which is primarily a religious organization, and the National States' Rights Party, which was indisputably a *bona fide* political party, contesting elections, and receiving a non-trivial share of the vote on several occasions. A large number of groups, although they do not contest elections, engage in open political activities such as holding meetings or publishing newsletters. Somewhat reluctantly, most Klan organizations are included in the category of above-ground organizations, since they do have addresses, newsletters and in some respects operate openly.[6] The extent to which organizational leaders direct or merely encourage terrorist actions is controversial. For example, the assassination of Malcolm X by three black Muslims is generally regarded as having been officially ordered, but exactly by whom is uncertain. The police believed that the order originated at the highest levels of the Nation of Islam, but had only circumstantial evidence for their belief (Goldman 1979: 314). Whether Elijah Muhammad himself handed down an edict calling for the killing can never be known. He certainly allowed his representatives to issue thinly veiled death threats, and told one follower that hypocrites like Malcolm X should have their heads cut off. To those Muslims who regarded him as a divinely inspired messenger "such a comment was more of a directive than an observation" (Clegg 1997: 219).

Members of extremist, but non-terrorist, groups are responsible for 27 percent of the incidents and 55 percent of the killings attributed to

4.2 Terrorist incidents and killings per 1,000 members of extremist
:ations

Organization	Incidents	Killings
Black Panther Party	32	14
Neo-Nazi groups	17	11
Jewish Defense League	5	a
Klans	3	1
Marxist	3	a
Black Muslim cults	2	1

Note
[a] Less than 0.5 per 1,000. All statistics rounded to the nearest whole number.

specific organizations. However, in relation to the size of their total
membership, most of these groups have very low rates of violence.
Table 4.2 shows the rate of violence for different extremist groups,
expressed as the number of incidents and killings per thousand
members. Even these statistics exaggerate the extent to which members
of extremist groups are prone to engage in violence, since many groups
avoid violence altogether. George and Wilcox (1992) list scores of
extremist groups active in the United States since the 1960s, with an
aggregate membership totaling well over 600,000. Yet the number of
incidents attributed to members of these groups is less than 300, indicating that the overwhelming majority of extremists never engage in
violence.

Terrorism by terrorist groups

In addition to terrorism involving extremist organizations, there is
terrorism carried out by terrorist groups (i.e. covert groups whose
sole purpose is terrorism). The great majority of such groups are
small, short-lived, and responsible for only a handful of incidents.
For the groups on which information is available, the median membership is ten, the group is active for less than two years, and carries out
seven attacks. The means are somewhat higher: fifty-two members, a
life of three years and sixteen attacks.[7] The means are higher than
the medians because of a handful of groups, who are able for whatever
reason to recruit more members, survive longer and carry out more
attacks. These relatively successful groups are listed in Table 4.3.

Since terrorist groups are set up specifically to engage in violence, it
is not surprising that their members are responsible for more acts of

Table 4.3 Major terrorist groups in America, 1955–2000

Group	Members	Incidents (killings)
White Knights (1964–68)	200	300 (9)
Weather Underground (1969–75)	300	38
Black Liberation Army (1971–82)	100	48 (10)
Mau Mau (1972)	50	6 (9)
FALN (1972–78)	25	150 (6)
Death Angels (1973–74)	19	22 (16)
New World Lib. Front (1974–78)	40	100 (3)
United Freedom Front (1975–84)	12	32 (1)
Macheteros (1978–86)	300	18 (7)
The Order (1982–85)	24	21 (4)

violence – relatively speaking – than members of extremist organizations. It is said that it doesn't take many people to carry out a terrorist
campaign, and in a literal sense this is true. The twenty-seven terrorist
groups for which we have size estimates were responsible for at least
643 attacks, and since the combined membership of the twenty-seven
groups comes to a (suspiciously precise) total of 1,405, this suggests a
rate of 458 attacks per thousand terrorists.

Typically, terrorist groups originate as splits from extremist mass
movements, or are made up of radicalized ex-members of such movements. Most revolutionary leftist groups had their ultimate origin in
the SDS, including most directly the Weathermen, and the United
Freedom Front. The founders of the Symbionese Liberation Army
were closely associated with the Venceremos, a Maoist group that
had been the largest and most activist radical movement in northern
California in the early 1970s (McLellan 1977: 58). A second generation
of terrorist organizations can trace their origins to members of these
organizations, with the New World Liberation Front including individuals who had been involved in the Symbionese Liberation Army,
while the M19 Communist Organization included remnants of the
Weather Underground. The Black Liberation Army broke away from
the Black Panthers in 1971, and the Death Angels were an offshoot
of the Black Muslims. Many members of the Order had previous connections with Aryan Nations and its religious affiliate, or to other
Christian Identity congregations (Barkun 1994: 231). In other cases,
informal links served as the basis of group formation: the Mau Mau
were a group of ex-Vietnam veterans, while the New Years Gang consisted of two brothers and two of their friends. The Macheteros were
founded by three Puerto Rican students after they had been to Cuba.

Almost all of the anti-abortion terrorist groups consisted of a handful of friends.

Some groups carry out a few attacks and are never heard of again, but eventually most are broken up by the police. The length of time a group is able to survive without being caught may reflect luck as much as anything else. The Symbionese Liberation Army, one of the most incompetent and bizarre urban guerrilla organizations that has appeared on the American scene, lasted for almost eighteen months.

Organizational ideologies and terrorist campaigns

Terrorists attack targets for ideological reasons. Indeed, it is their social and political objectives that serve to define them as terrorist attacks. In Table 4.4 the distribution of targets for each of the main waves of terrorism (by southern racists, black nationalists, black cults, revolutionary leftists, Puerto Rican *independistas*, and the contemporary extreme right) is shown. The pattern of targets for each group is distinctive, and in most instances the selection of targets is explained by the group's ideology. To put it another way, ideology serves as the organizing principle for terrorist campaigns. The large proportion of attacks classified as "other" include robberies and attacks on informers and factional rivals. Such actions will be discussed in the next section. Klan terror in the south was intended to intimidate blacks from exercising their civil rights and was moderately selective; although many of their victims were randomly selected blacks, almost half were civil rights workers, NAACP officials, and other activists.

Table 4.4 Distribution of terrorist attacks, by target and group ideology (%)

Target type	Sseg	Bnat	Bcult	Left	Indep.	Right
Foreign	–	1	–	6	–	–
Racist	88	1	66	–	–	60
Government	–	–	–	9	11	4
Police/Courts	1	66	12	10	10	8
Military	–	–	–	9	14	–
Liberal/Left	8	–	–	–	–	5
Conservative	–	–	–	1	1	–
Business	–	1	–	41	38	–
Utilities	–	1	–	7	12	1
Public places	–	–	–	2	6	3
Other	3	30	22	15	8	19

Black nationalists such as the Black Panthers saw the police as their main enemy. According to one Black Panther official,

> In our 400 year struggle for survival it has been the guns and force manifested in the racist pig cops that occupy our communities that directly oppress, repress, brutalize and murder us. . . . So when a self-defense group moves against this oppressive system, by executing a pig by any means, sniping, stabbing, bombing, etc., in defense against the 400 years of racist brutality and murder this can only be defined correctly as self-defense.

Cartoons in *The Black Panther* newspaper depicted black guerrillas with guns, and police officers shot down in a hail of bullets. Eldridge Cleaver declared that "a dead pig is the best pig of all. We encourage people to kill them, because the police constitute an army" (Heath 1976: 172–5).

Although black nationalist groups saw the police (including black police officers) as the enemy, black religious cults saw whites in general as the enemy. The theology of the Nation of Islam portrayed whites as devils created by the evil scientist Yakub, and this theme was constantly repeated in speeches and sermons. Several times black Muslim splinter groups took the idea seriously. The Death Angels in San Francisco earned their wings by murdering randomly selected whites, with a bonus for killing women or children. Members of the Yahweh cult in Miami brought back the ears of white vagrants as trophies.[8]

To the Puerto Rican *independistas*, the struggle against US colonialism involved a two-front war, in the United States and on the island. The mainland bombing campaign of the FALN was directed against banks, the corporate headquarters of organizations with economic interests in Puerto Rico, and other symbols of US capitalism and imperialism. In 1977, for example, the FALN bombed the FBI's New York offices and Department of Defense facilities, Sears, Marshall Fields, and Mobil. An August 1977 communiqué stated that "these corporations, which are part of Yankee imperialism, are the cause of the problems of the Puerto Rican people on the island and in the United States: since they are the ones that strangle us with their colonial yoke" (Fernandez 1994: 214).

Several of their most deadly attacks were carried out in retaliation for what the *independistas* believed was violence against them (Sater 1981: 5). The bombing of the Fraunces Tavern in New York on January 24, 1975, took place two weeks after the bombing of an *independista* rally in Puerto Rico. The FALN communiqué left at the

64 The organizational dynamics

site stated that the bombing was "in retaliation for the CIA-ordered bomb that murdered two innocent young workers who supported Puerto Rican independence. . . . We warned the North American Government that to terrorize and kill our people would mean retaliation by us." On the island, the Macheteros attacked US military personnel and other symbols of US colonialism. On December 9, 1979, they opened fire on a Navy bus, killing two sailors and wounding ten others. A communiqué justified their attack as a response to the alleged murder of Angel Rodriguez Cristobal, a Puerto Rican imprisoned for trespassing on the American naval base at Vieques.[9]

Revolutionary terrorists saw their enemies as the capitalist ruling class and their agents, hence they attacked corporations, banks, and the police. The Weathermen and other leftists selected their targets for symbolic reasons, and in only a handful of cases did they deliberately use deadly force. One of the rare exceptions was the assassination of Marcus Foster, the head of the Oakland school system, by the Symbionese Liberation Army.[10]

The contemporary wave of right-wing terrorism can be characterized ideologically in several ways – neo-Nazi, Christian Identity, survivalist, anti-government, etc. – and most groups embody various combinations of these ideological strains (Pearlstein 1991: 134). Racism and anti-semitism are common elements, and the majority of attacks (60 percent) have been directed against racial minorities and mixed-race couples. A flier, headed "Race Traitors," distributed by the Aryan Nations in the 1980s, announced that miscegenation was race treason, and that those involved would be punished by death (Kaplan 1997: 55). Aryan Nations and Christian Identity both see the United States as controlled by the "Zionist Occupational Government." Unlike the earlier wave of southern Klan violence, when several sheriffs and their deputies were Klan members, the new groups are extremely hostile to the police and have killed several officers (Melnichak 1986). There is an apocalyptic religious element to the antisemitic rhetoric of some groups. The Covenant, Sword, and Arm of the Lord (CSA) declared that "the planet earth is about to become the battleground between the forces of God . . . and Satan and his seed, the satanic blood-line Jews and those who have been deceived or bought off." Gordon Kahl, the North Dakota farmer and Posse Comitatus member who killed two federal marshals in 1983, wrote that "our nation has fallen into the hands of alien people. . . . These enemies of Christ have thrown our Constitution and our Christian Common Law into the garbage can" (cited in Barkun 1994: 206, 216, 231). However, despite the rhetoric of striking at the so-called Zionist Occupational Government, no elite Jews in government, business, or the media have been attacked, and there have been relatively few terrorist attacks against Jewish targets.[11] Leonard Weinberg (personal communication) suggests that this is because antisemitism is an esoteric element of the ideology. Most recruits are attracted to extreme right-wing groups because of their hostility towards racial minorities, and only after they have joined do they learn that Jews are the "real enemy."

Table 4.4 doesn't show the targets of the minor waves of terrorism, but these are also largely explained by ideology. Both Cuban and Jewish terrorism were primarily directed against foreign targets. Cuban *émigrés* attacked Cuban diplomatic targets and the embassies of those countries which opened diplomatic relations with Cuba, while members of the Jewish Defense League (JDL) bombed Soviet and Arab targets. Cuban extremists also targeted members of their own community. "They bombed Little Havana travel agencies, shipping companies, and pharmacies that conducted commercial transactions with Cuba," and murdered several *émigrés* who advocated coexistence with Castro (Garcia 1996: 141). The JDL murdered, or attempted to murder, suspected Nazi war criminals.

Anti-abortion terrorism provides an example of extreme target selectivity, since all the targets were either abortion clinics or individuals involved in abortion. In contrast Islamic terrorists have been willing to carry out attacks against the general public and individuals selected on the basis of ethnicity. In addition to the attacks of September 11 and the 1993 bombing of the World Trade Center, a bus carrying Hasidic students was fired upon in 1994. Islamic extremists assassinated Robert Kennedy in 1968, Rabbi Meir Kahane in 1990, and two CIA employees in 1993.[12]

Organizational needs and factional feuds

Not all terrorism is ideologically driven. Crenshaw (1988) points out that some terrorist activity, such as robberies to obtain funds or supplies, rescuing imprisoned comrades, or punishing informers, will be the result of organizational needs rather than ideology. Robberies by terrorist groups are certainly undercounted. Many – if not most – terrorist groups support themselves by robberies, and it is usually only after the group is captured (and not always then) that the robberies can be attributed to them. According to Mizell (1998: 12) over "the past twenty years, dozens of terrorist groups have robbed at least 368 banks and armored cars," which, along with punishing informers and attempted and successful rescues, would mean that perhaps one in ten actions carried out by terrorists should be seen as a response to organizational considerations.

   Self-interested acts by a terrorist group cannot be too numerous, or the distinction between political terrorism and common crime will be hard to maintain. As Richard Williams, a member of the United Freedom Front, argued "What differentiates us from criminals – what makes us political prisoners – is that criminal action is done for some type of personal gain." The United Freedom Front did rob banks, but it also bombed nineteen political targets, including a naval reserve center, a Navy recruiting office, two courthouses, and several corporate headquarters, thus justifying their claim to be "anti-imperialist freedom fighters." Some groups were definitely borderline. The George Jackson Brigade carried out fourteen robberies, and only eleven bombings. A detailed history of the prior career of one of the groups involved in the Brinks robbery by the M19 Communist Organization lists twenty-five robberies and only one political action – breaking Joanne Chesimard out of prison (Castellucci 1986). The terrorist, rather than merely criminal, nature of the Brinks robbery became apparent only after the political affiliations of those involved were revealed.

   Factionalism and organizational rivalries *within* ideological blocs often lead to violence, and although there is often an ideological element in such attacks, they are classified as a third category. Attacks on dissenters and apostates are most common in black separatist cults, presumably because of the threat such individuals pose to the legitimacy and authority structure of the organization.[13] When he left the Nation of Islam and derided Elijah Muhammad as a "religious faker," Malcolm X was first denounced and then assassinated. Seven Hanafi Muslims, including five young children, were massacred after their leader, Hamaas Abdul Khaalis, wrote to the ministers of all the Black Muslim mosques urging them to quit the sect and denouncing Elijah Muhammad as a "lying deceiver." A member of the Yahweh cult who criticized the group was beheaded. A large number of Black Panthers were beaten or killed in factional disputes (Anthony 1990: 131), and Pearson (1994: 188) describes the "campaign of intimidation" against ex-Panthers, and the fratricidal violence that followed the Newton–Cleaver split.[14]

   Table 4.5 presents another indicator of the relative importance of ideology, factional struggles and organizational imperatives: the number of deaths resulting from each type of action. Considering terrorism by organized groups as a whole, ideology explains the great majority of the killings (65.4 percent), with factionalism accounting

Table 4.5 Number of victims killed in different types of attack, by group ideology

Group	Ideological	Factional	Robbery	Informer	Other
Ku Klux Klan	27	1		2	
Black nationalist	36	8	4	3	4
Black cults	32	28	2	1	1
Leftist	1		4	2	2
Independistas	13		2		
Rightist	33			5	6
Total	142	37	12	13	13

for only 17.1 percent of the deaths, and robberies, killings of informers, and other organizationally related deaths, 17.5 percent.

Notes

1 The two previous acts of terrorism by *independistas*, the attack on Blair House in 1950 and the shots fired at the House of Representatives, were isolated incidents intended to draw attention to Puerto Rico's colonial status (Fernandez 1994: 80).
2 The figures for the years up to 1989 are given in Craig (1993: 51), and updated for subsequent years from the relevant issues of the *Washington Post*. The low turnout in 1987 is explained by a severe storm. Park Police stopped estimating the size of political rallies in 1997.
3 Seventy percent of white racist attacks were either unclaimed or not attributed to any specific group, as were 56 percent of leftist attacks and 48 percent of black militant attacks.
4 The skinheads were considered to be an informal group rather than an extremist or terrorist organization.
5 To make matters even more confusing, the BLA issued a communiqué in which they described the Brinks robbery as an action carried out by the Revolutionary Armed Task Force, under the leadership of the BLA.
6 The one significant exception is the White Knights of the Ku Klux Klan, set up in 1964 by Sam Bowers, which adopted a code of strict secrecy, "shunning the parades, rituals and other public displays that many Klans promoted" (Nelson 1993: 26–7).
7 The data in our chronology were supplemented by information in Degenhardt (1983), Janke (1983), George and Wilcox (1992), Mullins (1988), and Jongman and Schmid (1984).
8 The idea of whites as "devils" was plausible to many blacks, and as Clegg (1997: 134) points out, the appeal of Elijah Muhammad was linked with historical racism and segregation that "fed the flames of black discontent and made millenarianism and black separatism, even in their most extreme forms, an almost natural response for many African-Americans living under some of the worst conditions in the industrialized world."

9 Angel Rodriguez Cristobal was found hanging in his prison cell in Talla-hassee FL. He and several other activists occupied the shore of the naval base and weapons training complex. Photographs showed that he had been beaten (Fernandez 1987: 59–60).

10 According to their communiqué, the SLA "executed" Foster because he supported an identity card system for the schools which they considered to be racist.

11 Only eighteen of the 229 attacks by far right groups (8 percent) were against Jewish targets – resulting in four deaths. This includes one case where a man was killed by a neo-Nazi who thought he was Jewish, but excludes the incident in which five members of the Revolutionary Commu-nist Workers' Party were killed and eight wounded by neo-Nazis. This was considered to be a political target even though most of those killed were Jewish.

12 Between 1979 and 1991 the al Fuqra sect carried out a score of attacks on Hindus, Sikhs, and other Muslims. The group is led by a Pakistani cleric but has a predominantly black membership, and is not connected with Osama bin Laden.

13 Since Elijah Muhammad was seen as a prophet, attacks against him pre-sented "a danger that his ardent followers felt they needed to eliminate." Malcolm X demonstrated exactly how dangerous an enemy he could be by revealing details of Elijah Muhammad's extramarital affairs (Friedly 1992: 175).

14 After Elmer Pratt, deputy defense minister of the party, was expelled by Newton, his pregnant wife was tortured and murdered by Newton-faction Panthers (Pearson 1994: 308).

5   The terrorists

This chapter sets out to answer two questions: what *kind* of people become terrorists, and what is the *process* whereby they become terrorists? Two kinds of information will be used to answer these questions. Sociodemographic data are available for 818 named individuals who were indicted/arrested for terrorist crimes, were killed by police, or blew themselves up. For a smaller number (136) we have biographies which give more detailed and qualitative information. (A biography was defined as an account of an individual's life history, however brief.)

The sociodemographics of American terrorists

Of those whose age is given, the majority are under thirty, and there are few above fifty years old or below eighteen. Usually the age at the time of arrest and indictment are the same, but in the case of those who evade capture for a long time, the age when indicted is used. Although some types of terrorists are younger than others, in the aggregate they are not particularly youthful. The older terrorists are often the leaders, and leaders tend to be noticeably older than their followers. Overall about one in twelve (8.1 percent) of those indicted/arrested for terrorist offences are women, although this figure varies between different types, being highest for leftist revolutionaries, Puerto Rican *independistas*, and anti-abortionists, and lowest among the Cuban *émigrés*, Islamic extremists, and the Klan. In fact, no Cuban or Islamic terrorists were women, and the lone Klanswoman was unique in other respects, since she was the only Klan-affiliated individual to be killed by law enforcement during this early period.

Each group of terrorists has a distinct ethnic and occupational profile. The ethnic differences are the most obvious. Most of the groups can be defined, and define themselves, in ethnic or racial terms. The black groups were composed almost exclusively of blacks, the Jewish

Table 5.1 Percentage distribution by age of
those arrested for terrorist offenses

Age group	%
Under 18	4.0
18–29	50.1
30–39	25.4
40–49	13.1
50 or over	7.4
Total	100.0

groups of Jews, the anti-Castroites were all Cuban, and almost all the
independistas were Puerto Ricans.[1] The Klan members, drawn from
the rural south, were predominantly of Anglo-Saxon or Scotch-Irish
descent. It is interesting that the contemporary extreme right wing
mainly recruits from the same ethnic constituency as the Klan, albeit
on a national scale. In fact, using last name as the criterion, 97 percent
of the Klan were Anglo-Saxon/Scotch-Irish, 1 percent were German,
and 2 percent were from southern or eastern Europe, while among
contemporary right-wingers the comparable proportions are 82 percent, 11 percent, and 7 percent.[2] Given the nativist ideology common
to both groups, the continuing dominance of the Anglo-Saxon/
Scotch-Irish element is not surprising. The greater proportion of
German-American and other non-British descent individuals within
the New Right can be explained by the fact that the movement has
united two previously hostile elements, the Klan and the neo-Nazis
(Langer 1990). The contemporary "Aryan" movement emphasizes

Table 5.2 Age and sex of terrorists, by ideology of
group

Ideology	Median age	% women
Klan/segregationist	31	1.0
Black militant	24	9.4
Leftist revolutionary	27	22.3
Puerto Rican	34	20.0
Cuban	38	0.0
Jewish	26	7.4
Anti-abortion	32	19.5
New Right	30	3.4
Islamic	27	0.0

the links between the northern European peoples, and according to Christian Identity theology all are descendants of the lost tribes of Israel. Thus the ideology has a wider appeal than the nativism of the Klan.

Although one would expect the membership of the previously mentioned terrorist organizations to be drawn from a particular ethnic group, even members of groups that have no manifest ethnic or racial identity are far from being a random cross-section of the American population. The leftist terrorists were predominantly white,[3] and at least 26 percent were Jewish – ten times what would have been expected on the basis of the Jewish proportion of the American population.[4] This disproportionate involvement presumably reflects the historical radicalism of American Jews. Rothman and Lichter (1982) note that Jews made up a majority of the campus radicals in the 1960s, the milieu from which leftist terrorism emerged. All the anti-abortion extremists were white, although religion would appear a more relevant factor than ethnicity, since they were all highly religious (Blanchard and Prewitt 1993: 208).[5] Similarly, the most obvious feature of the Islamic radicals is that they are devout Muslims.[6]

There are also differences between the groups in terms of class and occupation. The Klan was a largely working-class group, with a handful of small business owners, self-employed and white-collar workers. The well-to-do and educated middle-class professionals were conspicuously absent from their ranks. Those indicted for the 1964 murder of three civil rights workers would seem fairly representative. They included four truck drivers, two salesmen, a mechanic, a restaurant owner, a Baptist minister, a building contractor, a gas station owner, and a construction worker. The leader of the group, Sam Bowers, was a coin machine distributor.

Ironically, members of the Weathermen and other revolutionary groups which sought to overthrow the *status quo* were generally from socially privileged backgrounds. They were the sons and daughters of corporate executives, lawyers, and other professionals, who had gone to prestigious elite schools. For example, the three Weathermen who perished in a March 1970 explosion, which destroyed a Greenwich Village town house, were graduates of Bryn Mawr, Columbia, and Kenyon College, while the two survivors were graduates of Swarthmore and Bryn Mawr. Only a minority came from blue-collar or lower white-collar backgrounds. The Puerto Rican nationalists were similar to the revolutionary leftists. They were a highly educated group; almost all had college degrees, and several had MAs or PhDs.

:cupationally they included teachers, a pharmacologist, and a television producer.

The black militants were drawn primarily from lower working-class backgrounds. A number could even be described as belonging to the underclass or lumpenproletariat, having been career criminals and/or drug addicts before joining the Black Panthers or the Nation of Islam. This is not surprising, since both organizations deliberately recruited on the streets and in the prisons. A number are described as unemployed veterans – or simply as veterans, without any indication that they were currently employed. However, the Panthers and other revolutionary nationalists differed from the black Muslims in their ability to attract a minority of college-educated middle-class individuals. The New African Freedom Fighters arrested in October 1984 were led by a *cum laude* graduate of Harvard, and the eight defendants and their spouses held "a total of ten college degrees and six postgraduate degrees, including three in law, two in education, and one in medicine." Except for the leader of the group, who was working towards his doctorate, all were employed. One woman held a clerical job, the others were professionals or civil servants (Larsen 1985).

The reported occupations of contemporary right-wing terrorists are very diverse. They include engineers, scientists, small business owners, soldiers, electricians, plumbers, house painters, factory workers, gas station attendants, and petty criminals. The anti-abortionists are typically lower middle-class or working-class. Table 5.3 summarizes the occupational/class profile of the different terrorist types. Given the small sample sizes, a simple threefold classification is used: socially advantaged, intermediate, and socially disadvantaged.[7] The first category includes upper middle-class professionals and above, the last semiskilled and unskilled blue-collar workers, while the intermediate category includes other white-collar and small-business occupations.

Table 5.3 Class profile of terrorists, by ideology (%)

Ideology	Advantaged	Intermediate	Disadvantaged
Puerto Ricans	69.2	7.8	23.0
Leftists	63.8	8.6	27.6
Black nationalists	26.5	8.8	64.7
New Right	22.5	20.0	57.5
Black cults	12.1	24.2	63.6
Anti-abortion	10.0	30.0	60.0
Klan	–	25.6	74.4

These patterns are generally consistent with previous research on the class and educational background of different types of terrorists. Studies of foreign terrorism found leftists, such as the Tupamaros of Uruguay and the German Red Army Faction, to be drawn from the educated middle class (Porzecanski 1973; Becker 1978). Similarly, a study of American terrorists in the 1980s (Smith 1994: 47) found that left-wing terrorists included many professional workers, with a majority (54 percent) having a college degree. Among right-wing terrorists only 12 percent had a college degree, and they included a "large number of unemployed or impoverished self-employed workers."[8]

Given the diverse occupational background of American terrorists, obviously no single factor can explain their resort to terrorism. Social deprivation supposedly explains why many blacks joined the Black Panthers or the Black Muslims, but why then were the white radicals from upper middle-class backgrounds? Most explanations of right-wing radicalism see it as a reaction to some kind of socioeconomic threat. Vander Zanden (1960) sees the Klan revival of the late 1950s as resulting from the status insecurities and frustrations of poor whites.[9] The rise of Posse Comitatus is explained as a response to the agricultural crisis of the 1980s (Burghart and Crawford 1996). Militia members are described by Berlet as "people who had good industrial jobs but have seen those jobs vanish," and who are threatened by "the social liberation movements of the 1960s . . . unhappy having to share power with people of color, with women . . . with the demands of the ecology movement, the gay and lesbian movement" (cited by Gay 1997: 12–13). According to Blanchard and Prewitt (1993: 209), the occupations of the anti-abortion extremists "isolate them from the tempering effects of work life in America," and they are socially marginal in their "integration into modern urban life." However, these theories are too broad-brush, with little predictive power. There were millions of disadvantaged young black males but only a few hundred engaged in political violence. Millions of white males fit Berlet's description, but only a handful have joined violent militia groups.

Psychological factors

The unusual nature of terrorism – in the sense that so few people carry out terrorist acts – suggests that terrorists are different from ordinary people. The earliest theory explaining why people become terrorists was a psychological one – there was a "terrorist personality." This is still a popular folk explanation: terrorists are in some way psychologically disturbed. The criminal justice system is predisposed to define terrorists as crazy rather than give them a platform to expound their views. When the 1993 World Trade Center bombers were allowed to make statements prior to being sentenced, their politically charged remarks were rebuked by the angry judge. In several cases, even against their clients' wishes, defense lawyers have claimed that their clients were mentally unstable. Sirhan Sirhan's attorney strongly opposed any attempt to address his political motives in killing Robert Kennedy, despite the fact that Sirhan repeatedly stated that it was because of Kennedy's support for Israel (Clarke 1982). Theodore Kaczynski, the unabomber, wanted to represent himself rather than having to endure his lawyers describe him as mentally ill. His request was denied by the judge, who ruled that it was the lawyers' choice rather than the defendant's whether or not to present a mental status defense. The judge acknowledged that Kaczynski appeared lucid and calm, and the court-appointed psychiatrist found Kaczynski competent to stand trial and competent to represent himself. Although the psychiatrist also offered a provisional diagnosis of paranoid schizophrenia, as one skeptic points out, "There is no credible evidence that he hears voices, has hallucinations or is out of touch with reality – unless reality is defined as having conventional social and political views" (Finnegan 1998: 61).

Even if not clinically crazy, terrorists are often stereotyped as social failures. When asked to explain his act, the ex-wife of a bomber of a gay night club answered: "Why did he do it? I think basically they're all losers, people who can't make it click and need something to blame their failures on" (*Seattle Times* November 11, 1990). The *New Yorker* dismissed Terry Nichol's life as "a catalog of failure. He was a flop as a farmer, a real-estate salesman, and soldier, and also as a husband." *Time* magazine explained that Buford Furrow, who shot up a Jewish child care center, was "down on his luck and mad at the world." According to an FBI official, angry rightists like Buford "are basically a bunch of losers who have to find someone they hate more than themselves" (*Time* August 23, 1999).

Are American terrorists psychologically disturbed, socially unstable individuals? Although we lack the detailed information to make such evaluations in the majority of cases, biographical data are available for a reasonably large number (136) of known terrorists. Only a small number are described as having personality disorders. Among the exceptions are Sam Brown of the Black Liberation Army and Cinque

DeFreeze of the Symbionese Liberation Army. Brown had an acute psychotic episode while being examined by the prison psychiatrist, and was diagnosed as having a schizoid personality disorder (Castellucci 1986: 243). DeFreeze had an early history of mental disturbance and while in prison was diagnosed as a paranoid schizophrenic (Parry 1976: 354–5). Byron de la Beckwith, the killer of Medger Evers, was an orphan and had been abused as a child. According to one psychoanalyst, Beckwith shared a number of traits with other political assassins; these included impotence and wife abuse, and having grandiose fantasies (Massengill 1994: 310–11). Four anti-abortionists appear to have had personality disorders. Peter Burkin was found not guilty by reason of insanity, and diagnosed as a schizophrenic. Joseph Grace was delusional – he was fleeing Norfolk, believing that a nuclear attack by Soviet Russia was imminent, when he decided to set fire to an abortion clinic. Robert Farley was a schizophrenic who had attempted suicide twice. Although sentenced to two consecutive life sentences, with no chance of parole, John Salvi was clearly delusional. He wanted the Vatican to provide financial aid to all poor Catholic families by issuing its own currency, and believed that the Freemasons were carrying out a program to sterilize Catholic girls (Swartz 1997). Among contemporary rightists two, Perry Warthan and Buford Furrow, seem deranged. As a thirteen-year-old Warthan murdered a ten-year-old, but was found not guilty by reason of insanity. He later had contacts with Charles Manson. Furrow was jailed after brandishing a knife at a psychiatric hospital, and had been on medication for several months before going on a shooting rampage. Steve Rombom of the Jewish Defense League spent eight years in psychiatric institutions.

Occasionally, psychiatrists disagreed as to the appropriate diagnosis, as in the case of Roy Moody. Jenkins (1997) notes that "psychiatric interviews were not a new experience for Roy Moody." On different occasions, he had been assessed as mature and stable, as schizophrenic, and as a sociopath. His final evaluation by the court-appointed psychiatrist concluded that he had sociopathic tendencies, so he has been included in the total.

Some extremists are accused of being crazy, but the evidence of their craziness seems to be that they hold extremist beliefs. Nelson (1993) says that the FBI agents who kept Sam Bowers (the head of the White Knights Klan group) under surveillance joked that he was an "unasylumed lunatic." However, all that Nelson offers in support of this claim is that Bowers was "an oddball with fixed routines [who] ate three meals a day seven days a week" at the same snack bar in his home town, and that "Bowers was thought odd by even his friends. He related to people almost solely on the basis of ideology." Richard Snell was diagnosed by his court-appointed psychiatrist as suffering from a paranoid delusional disorder, the symptoms of which were that he believed the US government to be controlled by Jews. Since this is one of the core beliefs of Aryan nationalists, it would be strange if he *did not* believe it. It is hard to escape the sense that we are being offered political or moral judgements disguised as psychiatric evaluations, so I have not included Bowers or Snell as psychologically disturbed.

Even if we consider other indicators of social maladjustment and social failure, the great majority of those in our sample seem normal, as Table 5.4 shows. A few had dropped out of college, had frequent job changes, or suffered business failures, but most had not. A handful had suffered abuse as children, done drugs, or drank heavily, but most had not. With the exception of the black militants, of whom about a third had been in prison, only 13 percent had a criminal history. One indicator often used as a sign of social and psychological stability is being married, and 43.5 percent of the sample were married – close to the national average.[10] These findings as to the normality of most terrorists agree with the assessments of others who have studied terrorists. Blanchard and Prewitt (1993: 208) note that "character witnesses [for anti-abortionists] invariably described them as good, hard-working, normal people." Flynn and Gerhardt (1989: 6) remark that few members of the Silent Brotherhood "possessed the emotional characteristics outsiders attribute to racists. There was a drifter here, an embittered loner filled with hate there. But they were outnumbered by people who had abandoned careers, families, and lives filled with promise to follow the cause. Only one . . . had done prison time."

Table 5.4 Terrorists and maladjustment

Characteristic	%
Psychologically disturbed	8.1
College dropouts	7.4
Economic failures	10.3
Alcohol/substance abusers	4.4
Criminals	19.1

Becoming a militant

How then do people become terrorists? Although, as noted in the previous chapter, most extremists *do not* engage in violence, most people who engage in political violence *have* been involved in extremist movements. More than half the individuals in the sample have a history of such involvement, and this is the case for all ideological categories. Contacts between extremists are likely to reinforce and increase their militancy, and also provide them with opportunities to organize. As Dees (1996: 200) argues, "militia groups attract those with a propensity for violence and act as a springboard for their activities. . . . They bring together like-minded people who may embolden one another and go on to form their own secret cell."

Involvement in an extremist movement is an example of a more general process that explains why some people become terrorists. Stark (1996) in a study of how people became Moonies concluded that converts were drawn into the group by social networks. Becoming a Moonie and becoming a terrorist are both examples of deviant behavior, and, like the Moonies, terrorists are recruited through social contacts. Aho (1990) found that among right-wing extremists "people first affiliate with right-wing activists and only then begin altering their intellectual outlooks to sustain and strengthen these ties. The original ties may develop from their jobs, among neighbors, among prison acquaintances, or through romantic relations." In their history of the Silent Brotherhood, Flynn and Gerhardt (1989) describe how several individuals joined the group because they knew and trusted Robert Mathews. For example, "Ken Loff began to take Bob Mathews' counsel on many things. It started slowly and grew steadily from the day Bob called him in California about purchasing the gasoline station. Loff trusted Mathews implicitly, so in casual conversation, when Bob started to talk more and more about race, Ken didn't question it." Another member, David Lane, "was contacted by his sister. . . . She was engaged to Carl Franklin, the Pennsylvania state leader of Aryan Nations. Lane's association with Franklin and his sister deepened his commitment to the white supremacist philosophy" (1989: 83, 215). Family connections underlie the recruitment of several Puerto Rican terrorists, with their biographies often noting that they came from a "family with a rich history of resistance to colonialism" or had "married into an *independista* family." Similarly, Klan involvement often seems to be inherited. Those arrested are frequently described as brothers, cousins, or even fathers and sons. One observer of a Klan rally remarked: "My attention was drawn to the number of

Social link	%
Involvement in extremist groups	55.9
Marriage	12.5
Significant other	6.6
Blood relatives	14.7
Other kin/in-laws	2.2
Occupational	8.1
Friendship/other social links	13.2

children there, and I suddenly began to understand the staying power of the KKK and how it was transmitted from one generation to another, like some hereditary disease" (Stanton 1991: 36). Table 5.5 shows that a high proportion of terrorists were linked through marriage and family connections, or other social relationships before engaging in terrorism. In a few cases, individuals became terrorists because of anger at perceived mistreatment or injustice. One black terrorist, Ben Chaney, was the younger brother of a murdered civil rights worker. Several white terrorists saw themselves as victims of affirmative action or desegregation.

Loners and crazies

American terrorism differs from terrorism in other countries in that a significant proportion of terrorist acts have been carried out by unaffiliated individuals rather than by members of terrorist organizations. Overall, if the Oklahoma City bombing is excluded, about one in six (15 percent) of all terrorist victims have been killed by unaffiliated individuals. Furthermore this type of terrorism is of growing importance. During the period from 1955 to 1977 such killings accounted for only 7 percent of the total, but during 1978–99 the proportion rose to 26 percent. If the Oklahoma City bombing is included, a *majority* of deaths after 1978, but before September 11, resulted from terrorism by unaffiliated individuals.

Eric Rudolph, who has been charged with the 1998 bombing of an Alabama abortion clinic, and is suspected of being involved in the 1997 bombing of a gay bar, and the 1996 bombing of Olympic Park in Atlanta, is a good example of this new type of terrorist. As a teenager he attended with his mother a Christian Identity congregation, the "Church of Israel," and he had some contacts with the Aryan Nations movement in later years, yet federal officials acknowledge that he apparently acted alone (Suro 1998).

Many law enforcement officials and terrorism analysts think that such loners will pose the greatest threat to the security of the United States over the next few years, since they are hard to identify before they act, and – as in Rudolph's case – hard to track down afterwards. Freelancers are defined as individuals who are not members of a terrorist group, or members of an extremist organization acting under the orders of an official of the organization. A terrorist group is considered to consist of at least four individuals and to have carried out more than one attack. Somewhat hesitantly, skinheads are considered to be members of a terrorist group.[11]

Table 5.6 lists the freelancers chronologically within ideological orientation, and the number of victims attributed to each. An examination of the list reveals several things. This type of terrorism has greatly increased in recent decades, and a majority of the freelancers have been right-wing racists. In about three-quarters of the cases, the perpetrators have been lone actors, while in the remaining cases the violence was by couples or, more rarely, by three persons. The violence has been particularly deadly, with multiple victims in several cases. There were at least seven serial killers, and six single incidents in which more than one person was killed.

Table 5.6 Unaffiliated terrorist killers, by ideology and date

Right-wing racists		Islamic	
1963	Floyd Simpson (1)	1968	Sirhan Sirhan (1)
1963	Byron de la Beckwith (1)	1993	Mir Aimal Kansi (2)
1963	Michael Farley and Larry Sims (1)	1994	Rashid Baz (1)
1968	James Earl Ray (1)	*Black militants*	
1970–75	Neal Long (7)	1970	Ben Chaney, Linzie Rutrell (4)
1979–80	John Paul Franklin (15)		
1980	Joseph Christopher (13)	1972–73	Mark Essex (7)
1982	Frank Spisak (3)		
1983	Gordon Kahl (2)	*Anti-abortionists*	
1989	Roy Moody (2)		
1992	Randy Weaver (1)	1994	Paul Hill (2)
1996	Eric Rudolph (2)	1994	Michael Griffin (1)
1999	Benjamin Smith (2)	1994	John Salvi (2)
1999	Ben and James Williams (2)		
1999	Buford Furrow (1)		

Note
Number of victims killed shown in parentheses.

What are the characteristics of these unaffiliated terrorists? Although not members of terrorist groups, almost all of them are, or have been, involved with extremist groups. To take a recent example, Buford Furrow had been a member of Aryan Nations, lived for a while with Robert Mathews' widow, and investigators found Christian Identity literature in his home. Of the right-wingers listed in Table 5.6, two had previous or current links with the National States' Rights Party, two with the Klan, one with Posse Comitatus, four with Christian Identity, and three with the World Church of the Creator. Mark Essex, a black militant who killed seven whites, had been a member of the Republic of New Africa. Although most terrorists are normal, the rate of psychological disturbance is certainly higher among the loners, with at least six of the twenty-seven listed individuals showing symptoms of mental illness.[12]

Notes

1 The exceptions are so few that they can be listed by name. Marilyn Buck was the sole white member of the Black Liberation Army, and Paul Weinberg was the only non-Puerto Rican member of the Macheteros. Two Puerto Ricans (Francisco and Gabriel Torres) were members of the Black Liberation Army, and Jose Rios was a member of the New African Freedom Fighters. One JDL terrorist, Thomas MacIntosh, was a convert.
2 Two New Right terrorists, William and Ivan Wade, claimed to be American Indians.
3 Smith (1994: 49) describes them as largely composed of racial minorities, but this is only true if the black and Puerto Rican groups are included. Excluding these, only 4 percent were non-white.
4 Since most of those classified as Jewish were identified on the basis of their names, it is likely that this statistic is an underestimate. For example, despite his name, Sam Melville was Jewish. Handler (1990) also found a disproportionate number of Jews (19.2 percent) among left-wing American terrorists of the 1960s and 1970s.
5 Since blacks are more opposed to abortion than whites, their absence is surprising. According to one poll, 16 percent of blacks, compared with 10 percent of whites, thought abortion should always be illegal (*Gallup Poll Monthly* April 1991). The denominational breakdown includes Mormons, Pentecostals, Catholics, Lutherans, and Baptists.
6 By nationality, they included Palestinians, Egyptians, Lebanese, Sudanese, Pakistanis, and Afghans.
7 Those groups (the Jewish Defense League, Islamic, and Cubans) for which fewer than ten cases with occupation are known are ignored.
8 An earlier study by Handler (1990) also found that left-wing American terrorists were far more likely to be college-educated than right-wing terrorists (68 percent compared with 19 percent).

9 Vander Zanden's interpretation is based on his analysis of the occupations of 153 Klansmen, of whom one-third were unskilled or semiskilled, while two-thirds were in an intermediate position between the working and middle classes.

10 In 1980, 51.8 percent of the total population were married, while among males aged twenty-five to twenty-nine the figure was 43.8 percent.

11 Though one might consider skinheads to be loners held together by such diffuse ideological links as reading racist magazines, watching television programs and listening to White Power rock (Hamm 1993: 138–40).

12 This figure would be even higher if the lone gunmen (two blacks and two whites) responsible for a single massacre were included in the count. The two blacks were Colin Ferguson, who killed five people on a commuter train, and Roland Smith, who killed seven people in Harlem. The two whites were Patrick Purdy, who opened fire on a school playground, killing five Asian children, and Frederick Cowan, who killed four co-workers and a policeman. Smith, Purdy, and Cowan committed suicide, while Ferguson was found not guilty because insane.

6 Dealing with terrorists

In the United States, until recently, terrorism was regarded as a criminal matter, to be handled by the police, the FBI, and other law enforcement agencies. When caught, terrorists were tried in regular criminal courts, and there was no special crime of "terrorism." This chapter first examines how terrorists are killed or captured by police, then at how captured terrorists are treated by the criminal justice system. Law enforcement agencies have, on occasion, behaved in illegal, unconstitutional, and immoral ways, so this aspect of anti-terrorist policy will also be discussed. Finally, the effectiveness of anti-terrorist policies in stopping or reducing terrorism will be examined.

Killing terrorists

Police kill as well as capture terrorists, and the use of deadly force by police is not uncommon. Table 6.1 shows the number of terrorists and extremists, broken down by ideological type, who were killed by law enforcement personnel. The agencies responsible for such killings were city police (forty-six), the FBI (seven), sheriffs' departments (three), and state troopers (two). The table also shows the number of police killed by each group of terrorists, and it is interesting to note that the latter is similar to (and usually slightly higher than) the number of terrorists killed by the police. This parity between the two kinds of fatalities suggests that the police response was generally proportional to the danger they faced. Most of those shot by police were killed when police returned fire, or were apprehending suspects, or when individuals were behaving in a threatening manner.

There were, however, a few occasions in which it appears that police ambushed or assassinated political extremists. (The number of these suspicious fatalities is shown in parentheses.) The only member of the

Table 6.1 Number of terrorists and extremists killed by police

Ideological category	Killed by police	Police killed
Klan	1 (1)	1
Black militants	34 (3)	56
Black Muslims	3	4
Leftists	8	7
Puerto Ricans	2 (2)	5
Rightists	10 (2)	9

Note
Numbers in parentheses are numbers of suspicious killings by police.

Klan ever killed by police, Kathy Ainsworth, was shot to death in a police ambush, when she and Thomas Tarrants attempted to blow up a synagogue in Meridian MS. The ambush was set up by two Klansmen who had been bribed with money provided by the Anti-defamation League and the Mississippi Jewish community.[1] In a pre-dawn raid by Chicago police on an apartment occupied by Black Panthers, Fred Hampton and Mark Clark were killed and four other Panthers were wounded. Although police claimed that the Panthers fired first, forensic evidence showed that only one shot was fired by the Panthers and more than eighty by the police (and also suggested that Hampton had been asleep when he was killed). One other Panther, Bobby Hutton, was also killed under suspicious circumstances. After surrendering, he and Eldridge Cleaver were ordered to run to the squad car, whereupon Hutton was gunned down by the police. Epstein (1971) concludes, after a careful review of the evidence, that these were the only two cases when Black Panthers were killed by police whose lives were not being directly threatened.[2] In Puerto Rico, two *independistas* were ambushed by police on their way to bomb a police station; the two men were accompanied by a police informant, who had urged them to commit the act, and were gunned down without warning. The incident, which became known as the Cerro Maravilla affair, was at first covered up but then became a major issue in the 1984 elections and led to the defeat of the ruling New Progressive Party (Nelson 1986). During the Ruby Ridge siege of August 1992, Vicki Weaver was killed by an FBI sniper while she was holding her baby daughter. Her fourteen-year-old son, Sam, had been shot two days earlier. Her husband, Randy Weaver, was awarded $3 million after winning a wrongful death suit against the Justice Department (Bock 1995).

Surveillance, harassment, and arrests

Law enforcement may engage in heavy surveillance or virtually ignore extremist groups. Arrests may be selective or extensive. In this section the differences in the overall response to different waves of extremist violence are examined.

After the incident in which four Puerto Rican nationalists opened fire on the House of Representatives in 1954, the government responded by arresting large numbers of nationalists both in the United States and in Puerto Rico itself. Of the 179 persons who were arrested, most were subsequently released, and only twenty-one were tried (*Keesing's* 1954: 13683, 13898). After the robbery of a Wells Fargo depot in 1983 by the Macheteros, the FBI raided the homes of scores of independence activists in Puerto Rico. Thirty-seven *independistas* were arrested and subsequently released without charge, while those who were charged spent over two years in pretrial detention. Although ninety days is the maximum period for preventive detention, it was not until October 1986 that the US Court of Appeals ruled the continued pretrial detention of the defendants was unconstitutional (Fernandez 1987: 241). Until disbanded in 1987, the Intelligence Unit of the Puerto Rican police relied on a vast network of informers to maintain dossiers on at least 135,000 independence supporters. Information in the so-called *carpetas* was used to deny jobs and otherwise discriminate against alleged subversives.[3]

There is general agreement that the Black Panthers were subjected to nationwide harassment by police, and a special unit was set up in the Justice Department to coordinate federal and local police efforts against them (Goodell 1973: 118). A survey by the Associated Press found that in the twelve months from May 1969 to May 1970, 230 Panthers had been arrested, and also that, of the cases which had come to trial, only 40 percent resulted in convictions. According to Charles Garry, chief counsel for the party, from May 1967 to December 1969, 700 Panthers were charged with offenses ranging from murder and armed robbery to loitering and possession of marijuana. I analyzed these 700 arrests (which are reported in the February 21, 1970, issue of the *Black Panther* newspaper), and found that about half (48 percent) were for vaguely defined or trivial offenses such as disorderly conduct, loitering, passing out leaflets, etc., which might be reasonably regarded as harassment. Another 17 percent of the arrests were for ordinary criminal acts, including armed robbery, burglary, possession of stolen property, pimping, etc., while 12 percent involved weapons possession. The remaining cases, in which Panthers were charged with machine-gunning a police station, conspiring to bomb a police station, attempted murder of police, etc., were classified as political terrorism.[4]

Police raids on Panther offices were common, and those arrested were often released without being charged. In 1969 alone, there were raids in San Francisco, Los Angeles, Chicago, Detroit, Denver, Salt Lake City, Indianapolis, San Diego, and Sacramento (Zimroth 1974: 82–5). The effect of these arrests was to force the Panthers to spend their time raising money for bail and other legal expenses, thus diverting them from political organizing. Also, since bail was often denied or set so high, the arrests served as a form of preventive detention, thus further weakening the organization. For example, in the case of the "Panther 21" accused of conspiring to attack a New York police station, bail was set at $100,000 for each defendant, which meant that most of them spent up to two years in jail, awaiting trial.

In some countries, anti-terrorist efforts involve mass searches of hostile areas, in which civilians are stopped at random. This has occurred in America on at least *some* occasions – all involving blacks. During the Death Angels' reign of terror in San Francisco, police launched an all-out search throughout the black community, stopping and questioning hundreds of black men. Some individuals were stopped and asked for their identification as many as six times. The police invaded a movie theater, shone flashlights on the audience, then pulled out and searched half a dozen blacks.[5] After a New York City patrolman was murdered by the Black Liberation Army, Daley (1973: 418) describes how:

> out in the street, 9th Precinct cops were stopping every black man they saw. They brought in something like eight men whom they had stopped and taken guns from. None of these men proved to have anything to do with the assassination, and none of the arrests would stand up in court, for they were the results of illegal search and seizure.

Police responded in a similarly indiscriminate fashion in Cleveland and Baltimore after police were shot by black militants (Masotti 1969: 46).

While police action against Puerto Ricans and black militants may be plausibly attributed to racism, the Klan was also subject to heavy-handed surveillance by the FBI. Indeed, as George and Wilcox (1992) point out, most of the techniques used against black militants were first used against the Klan. Hoover boasted of how he dealt with the White Knights of the Ku Klux Klan: "There are 480 Klansmen in Mississippi. . . . I had our agents interview every member of the Klan there, just to let them know we know who they are." One account describes how the FBI "mounted an eleven-week war of nerves. . . . Agents kept watch on Bowers [the head of the group] virtually around the clock" ("Malice towards some" 1966: 40).

After the World Trade Center and Oklahoma City bombings, Congress granted increased powers to the FBI, and the federal government adopted a proactive policy aimed at preventing terrorist attacks by the surveillance of extremist groups. The goal is to uncover terrorist conspiracies while they are still in the planning stage. At the Justice Department, a task force holds biweekly meetings to evaluate intelligence reports and coordinate national strategy. Efforts have focused on two groups, Islamic fundamentalists and the far right. The new laws allowed the FBI to investigate individuals even if they were not suspected of any specific offense. Other laws, making it a crime to send money to foreign groups that the State Department classifies as terrorist, and allowing the government to detain or deport immigrants suspected of terrorist links, have been used almost exclusively against Muslim individuals and groups. Under the Foreign Intelligence Surveillance Act, the FBI carried out over 5,000 secret wiretaps during the 1990s. Civil libertarians are unhappy with the use of secret evidence in immigration cases, and claim that the FBI equates rhetoric with material support for terrorism, and that several of those prosecuted are victims of guilt by association ("US Muslims scrutinized in terror probes" 1998).

Since the task force was set up in late 1995, FBI investigations of right-wing extremists have increased more than fourfold. These investigations typically involve electronic surveillance and the use of undercover agents (Klaidman 1996). The number of right-wing extremists arrested has increased dramatically, with almost 300 being charged with various offenses since 1979. This figure (which is based on my own data set) is certainly an undercount, but what is striking is that over a third of those arrested had not yet committed any violent acts. Anecdotal evidence suggests that known right-wing extremists are under surveillance and harassed by police.[6]

What is striking about contemporary law enforcement activities directed against right-wing extremists is the involvement of self-appointed watchdog groups such as the Anti-defamation League (ADL) and the Southern Poverty Law Center (SPLC). These groups monitor racist and antisemitic groups and then share their information with law enforcement agencies, thereby giving government agencies a rationale for infiltrating the groups which they would otherwise have lacked. The ADL has lobbied for the passage of hate crime laws, and many states have adopted the ADL model statutes, which create new substantive offenses of "intimidation" and "institutional vandalism" and result in more severe punishments for existing crimes. Morris Dees, the founder of the SPLC, has made creative use of the common-law principle of "vicarious liability" to bring civil suits against national white separatist organizations on behalf of the victims of racist attacks. In 1987 Dees bankrupted the Alabama United Klans of America with a $7 million judgement for the family of Michael Donald, who was murdered by Klansmen. In 1990, after skinheads beat to death Mulugeta Seraw, Dees won a $12.5 million punitive damages settlement against White Aryan Resistance. In 1997 a $1 million judgement was handed down against two Klan groups after an interracial march in Georgia was stoned. In 1998 a South Carolina jury ordered two Klan chapters to pay $37.8 million – the largest-ever award in a hate crime case – for creating an atmosphere of hate that led to the arson of a black church. Most recently, a woman and her son were awarded $6.3 million against Aryan Nations leader, William Butler, because his security guards assaulted two passing motorists after their car backfired.[7] The result of this litigation was to bankrupt and silence these organizations, which was Dees's declared intent.[8]

One might argue that, in all the previously described cases, society responded vigorously – and in some cases overreacted – to major outbreaks of politically motivated violence. In other cases, however, the authorities were criticized for ignoring the violence or for not putting enough effort into stopping it. Abortion rights groups accused the Reagan administration of downplaying anti-abortion violence, when William Webster, the director of the FBI, refused to classify clinic bombings and arson as terrorism on the grounds that there was no evidence of an organized conspiracy. Subsequently, however, it would be difficult to make such an argument. The Freedom of Clinic Entrances Act of 1994 criminalized many anti-abortion protest tactics. The National Organization of Women successfully used the Racketeer Influenced and Corrupt Organizations statute (originally devised as a weapon against organized crime) to sue the leaders of Operation Rescue and the Pro-life Action League. Jurors awarded $86,000 to the two abortion clinics on whose behalf the suit had been brought. In 2001, a federal appeals court unanimously upheld the judgement, saying the demonstrators had gone beyond free speech when they "trespassed on clinic property and blocked access to clinics with their bodies, at times chaining themselves in the doorways of clinics or to operating tables." In 1999, an anti-abortion web site, the "Nuremberg Files," was closed down on the grounds that it encouraged attacks on abortion doctors. Abortion rights groups denounced the site as a "hit list" that incited violence against abortion clinics, and in a civil suit abortion providers won a $107 million settlement from a Portland OR jury in 1999. Two years later, a federal appeals court overturned the award, and ruled unanimously that the internet site was protected speech. The court concluded that "Political speech may not be punished just because it makes it more likely that someone will be harmed at some unknown time in the future by an unrelated third party" (Sanchez 2001: A1). Kaplan (1995) describes the harsh treatment of anti-abortion demonstrators by police and courts. Demonstrators have experienced extreme police brutality both when being arrested and when in jail. Heavy damages have been levied against them for trespassing.

The police were noticeably unsuccessful initially in dealing with Cuban *émigré* terrorism. One article claims that Cuban terrorism "constitutes a monumental (and peculiar) failure on the part of US investigative agencies. Eighty percent of the 100 and more bombings and killings in the Miami area since 1974 remain unsolved" ("Cuban exiles: Miami, haven for terror" 1977: 326). The FBI's inability to apprehend the white radicals of the 1960s was also commented on. According to an article in the *New York Times Magazine*, "Whatever its record with ordinary criminals, the FBI isn't too hot at catching the new breed of fugitive" (Lukas 1970). The white revolutionaries were difficult to catch for several reasons. They were college-educated, and could rely on a well organized and well financed network of supporters. This radical underground was difficult for the FBI to penetrate, due to the cultural gap between their agents and the student radicals.[9] In the case of the Jewish Defense League, the New York Police Department seems to have been remarkably unconcerned about the threat it posed, although the police did infiltrate two officers into the group (Rosenthal 2000). After the murder of Alex Odeh, an official of the American-Arab Anti-discrimination Committee, apparently by JDL members, there were complaints that the case was not being investigated vigorously. The FBI, however, claimed its investigations into this case and other bombings were hampered because many of the suspects had fled to Israel, and the Israelis were not cooperating with the FBI (Kurtz 1987).

Lack of success is not necessarily a result of lack of effort, since terrorist crimes are in many respects more difficult to solve than normal crimes, and some kinds of terrorists may be more difficult to catch. Table 6.2 gives, for each ideological category, the number of terrorists brought to trial and compares this with the seriousness of

Table 6.2 Number of incidents compared with number brought to trial, by ideological category

Category	Incidents	Arrests	Ratio
Rightists	245	275	1.12
Blacks	475	289	0.61
Klan	588	227	0.39
Jewish	115	41	0.36
Cubans	112	38	0.34
Puerto Ricans	383	85	0.22
Anti-abortion	202	43	0.21
Leftists	684	88	0.13

the threat from that category, as indicated by the number of attacks they carried out. There appears to be a somewhat disproportionate effort devoted to black militants and to the contemporary far right, while the lack of success in apprehending leftists is apparent.

How terrorists are caught

The agencies responsible for apprehending the terrorists were in order of importance: the FBI (44 percent), local police departments (41 percent), joint FBI and local police involvement (8 percent), state police (3 percent), with the remainder attributable to the Bureau of Alcohol, Tobacco and Firearms, sheriffs' departments, and (once) an off-duty correction officer. However, this hides variation according to terrorist type, with the FBI playing a major role in all types except in the case of the black militants, who were dealt with by local police departments.

How do police capture terrorists? Information is available for only a small proportion of cases, but some interesting patterns are suggested by an examination of the factors involved in identifying and apprehending them. Table 6.3 shows the relevant factors in the 293 cases for which details are available. The factors are classified under seven headings and, since some cases involved more than one factor, the percentages sum to more than 100.

The use of informers is one of the most common ways[10] in which terrorists are caught, and three types can be distinguished: where a group is infiltrated by a police agent, where a member of a group is "turned," usually after being arrested and offered a deal, and where an informant comes forward in response to a specific reward.[11] Reportedly, as many as sixty FBI agents infiltrated the Mississippi Klan, at a

90   *Dealing with terrorists*

Table 6.3 Most important factors involved in
the capture of terrorists (%)

Informers and infiltrators	46.4
Surveillance	29.7
Caught in the act	23.5
Routine policing	7.5
Investigation	14.7
Information from public	8.5
Fellow terrorists	2.4

time when it supposedly had less than 500 members. The murderers of
three civil rights workers were identified by a member of the police
department who joined the Klan in April 1964, and became an FBI
informer in September. The key witness in the case was a former Klansman, who told the FBI what he knew for $3,000, plus $100 a week for
the following year. The murderers of Violet Liuzzo were convicted on
the testimony of Thomas Rowe, Jr, a Klansman who had been on the
FBI's payroll for six years.[12] The murder of Willis Brewster, a black
man randomly shot to death, so shocked the town of Anniston that
the local newspaper and civic leaders raised over $20,000 for informa-
tion on his killers. Three men were subsequently indicted (Bullard 1989:
84–5).

    Black groups were heavily infiltrated by police agents. One Panther
complained how "the problem with most of these underground organizations was that the FBI and police were underground with them.
When they surfaced to perform some revolutionary act, it was usually
a setup, and the members of the organization were busted" (Anthony
1990: 26). When the New York chapter of the Black Panthers was
started, undercover police were among the founding members, and
six agents from the Bureau of Special Services of the NYPD gave
evidence during the trial of the Panther 21.[13]

    One of the agents, Ralph White, had joined the party before any of
the defendants. White was there when the two Panthers whose job it
had been to plant a bomb in the 44th Precinct stashed dynamite
behind a refrigerator at the Elsmere Tenants' Council, a Bronx anti-
poverty agency. He took the dynamite to police headquarters, where
the bomb squad substituted clay and oatmeal for it, thwarting the
44th Precinct bombing before it took place. Another agent, Eugene
Roberts, "so trusted by the Panthers that he penetrated their security
section, was sent out with another Panther to find the best places

to plant firebombs in four big New York City department stores"
(Castellucci 1986: 42–3).

Informants often identified suspicious vehicles or addresses for surveillance, or tipped off police that something was going to happen,
thus allowing a stakeout to be set up. After a tip from an informer,
the New Afrikan Freedom Fighters were placed under intensive FBI
surveillance. For nine months, the group was watched by up to 100
agents a day, and over 500 phone conversations were taped (Larsen
1985). In their efforts to capture Puerto Rican terrorists, FBI agents
"followed the revolutionaries by wiretapping their cars, wiretapping
their apartments, wiretapping the public telephones in front of their
homes, and even wiretapping people when they made love in the
shower" (Fernandez 1987: 245). Such wiretaps are obviously costly in
terms of money and manpower. For example, the wiretaps on the
Mutula Shakur group "ultimately cost $2 million, involved fifty
agents, and lasted 169 days" (Castellucci 1986: 261). The investigation
of the Macheteros, who robbed the Wells Fargo truck, cost $8 million –
more than the money taken in the robbery itself.

Large numbers of individuals were caught by police in the act of
committing terrorism, or while fleeing the scene. Such cases often overlap with, and are difficult to distinguish from, routine policing. Larry
Plamondon, a White Panther leader, and two companions were
stopped by a sheriff's deputy after throwing beer cans out of their
car. A quick check through the National Crime Information Center
identified two of them and the car was stopped for a second time, by
state police (Newton and Newton 1991). Two members of the M19
Communist Organization, responsible for the 1981 Brinks robbery,
were arrested after a police officer thought they looked suspicious
while unloading their truck at a public storage facility. A subsequent search of their storage bin turned up a cache of weapons and
explosives.

Under the heading of investigation are included arrests made as a
result of searches, questioning witnesses, matching and checking
records. Sometimes terrorists leave clues, whereby they can be traced
through diligent police work. In describing how a member of the
Black Liberation Army was apprehended, a police spokesman said,
"There was no miracle connected with our finding him – it was just
dog work. We checked out everything. Somebody said they saw him
playing basketball in Brooklyn. Somebody else heard he was at a
social club. We checked out everything" (Kaufman 1973: 10). A speed-
ing ticket and a fake driving license allowed the police to link together
several members of the BLA/M19CO alliance, and also led to the

discovery of their safe house. Patti Hearst and the surviving members of the Symbionese Liberation Army were tracked down after police identified a red Volkswagen which had been parked outside a Pennsylvania farmhouse which had been occupied by the fugitives. One particularly impressive example is provided by the capture of the Macheteros, who robbed a Brinks truck in Hartford CT. They were caught after the group had fired an antitank rocket at the federal building in Hato Rey, Puerto Rico. The abandoned getaway car was searched and, although it was registered under a false name and address, and had been wiped clean of fingerprints, a traffic ticket was found, squeezed into a side pocket. It was matched with a false driver's license, and the photograph on the license matched a man already under surveillance. He was then followed and led FBI agents to the rest of the cell (Fernandez 1987: 224–5). The robbery of an armored truck in Ukiah WA by the Order was solved in a similar fashion. A pistol left behind at the scene by one of the robbers was traced back to the gun shop where it had been sold. The buyer was identified, then all phone calls to the Montana–Idaho area from the motel (where he had stayed for the three days prior to the robbery) and nearby pay phones were traced. This linked the robbery with known members of Aryan Nations and other extremists. Searches of their homes turned up other names (Flynn and Gerhardt 1989: 261–5).

One fugitive, Joseph Cowan, suspected in a nationwide bombing conspiracy, was arrested after a fellow worker recognized him from newspaper and television pictures, and phoned the FBI. Marilyn Buck was arrested when buying guns for the BLA, after she gave two different names to the alert owner of a San Francisco gun store, who promptly notified the BATF (Castellucci 1986: 81). Ted Kaczinski, the unabomber, was turned in by his brother.

Under interrogation, criminals often turn in their cohorts in the hope of receiving more lenient treatment. Ideologically motivated individuals are less likely to do this, but some do. Three Klansmen, who had murdered a black army reserve lieutenant colonel, were implicated by another Klansman, who confessed under questioning. One anti-abortionist who was imprisoned without bail while awaiting trial for bombing an abortion clinic expected his pastor to see that his wife and children were taken care of during his incarceration. When the pastor suggested that the family go on welfare, the bomber agreed to testify for the state, and wore a wire in order to record several hours of conversation which incriminated the pastor in the bombing (Blanchard and Prewitt 1993: 203).

Terrorists in the criminal justice system

After the terrorists are caught, the prosecutors must decide what to charge them with, juries must decide whether to convict them of the charges, and if they are convicted judges must decide what sentences to impose. If the data were ideal, we could evaluate the effect of all these factors, case by case. However, it is still possible to discern some general patterns in how terrorists are treated compared with other criminals, and to compare different groups of terrorists to see whether certain groups are treated in a relatively harsh or lenient fashion.

Our sources identify 1,778 individuals suspected of terrorist crimes, in that they were arrested or sought by the police. Of these, 8 died while awaiting trial, 54 remained fugitives, 71 were awaiting trial, and in 116 instances, although the individuals were convicted, their sentence is unknown. For 852 individuals, the criminal justice outcome is reported. This leaves over 600 people who were arrested, but for whom no information as to their criminal justice outcomes is available.[14] This discrepancy is probably explained by the fact that most of those arrested were released without being charged. I assume that the cases in my data set, for which the criminal justice outcomes are known, constitute both the great majority of cases brought to trial, and a reasonably representative sample. The distribution of the known criminal justice outcomes is shown in Table 6.4. (Some individuals were tried more than once, so the total outcomes number 892, not 852.)

Several factors affect criminal justice outcomes. The low rate of conviction for black defendants shown in Table 6.5 probably reflects the fact that prosecutors appear to have "overcharged" black militants, and hence prosecuted some individuals when the evidence against them was too weak to obtain a conviction. Smith (1994: 178) points

Table 6.4 Criminal justice outcomes of all known cases (%)

Charges dropped/dismissed	9.5
Acquitted/verdict overturned	16.3
Mistrial	7.2
State's evidence	0.8
Fine/community service, etc.	3.9
Probation/suspended sentence	8.7
Prison sentence	52.2
Death sentence	1.2

out that this strategy "is commonly used to elicit a guilty plea on some counts in exchange for dropping numerous extraneous counts."

The composition of the jury may have played a role in the outcome of some trials. The first Black Panther trial before a predominantly black jury, and presided over by a black judge, resulted in the acquittal of twelve Panthers charged with the attempted murder of five New Orleans police officers. A Puerto Rican jury acquitted Filiberto Ojeda Rios, who had shot and blinded an FBI agent during his arrest, of all charges against him. Two trials of the BLA gunmen who shot a policeman to death ended in mistrials, apparently because of racial feelings on the part of the predominantly black jury. Southern juries were often biased and reluctant to convict Klansmen and others accused of racist attacks, even if the evidence indicated that they were guilty. This was especially apparent in the more serious cases, such as murder cases, and Byron de la Beckwith bragged that "no southern jury would ever convict a white man for killing a nigger." Currently, predominantly white juries do not seem to display any general sympathy for right-wing terrorists, although there have been some instances. For example, two years after the Ruby Ridge shoot-out, an Idaho jury found Kevin Harris and Randy Weaver not guilty of murdering US Deputy Marshall William Deegan, and also found Weaver not guilty of selling illegal shotguns – the offense which had provoked the whole incident. In 1981 in Chattanooga, of three Klansmen charged with shooting five elderly black women, two were acquitted by an all-white jury and one received a nine-month jail sentence.

Once convicted, it is possible that judges may sentence different types of terrorists differently. In the only previous study to examine this

Table 6.5 Criminal justice outcomes, by group ideology

Ideology	All offenses % convicted (n)	Deadly offenses % convicted (n)
Anti-abortion	100.0 (32)	100.0 (3)
Puerto Ricans	94.3 (53)	100.0 (3)
Rightists	87.6 (217)	80.8 (52)
Cubans	85.7 (21)	20.0 (5)
Left-wing	70.6 (85)	100.0 (20)
Jewish	69.2 (39)	20.0 (5)
Black militants	51.1 (268)	75.4 (118)
Klan	47.8 (180)	28.7 (87)
Average	63.9 (895)	62.8 (293)

issue, Smith (1994: 180), after analyzing the sentences of those identified as terrorists by the FBI in the 1980s, found that "there is little variation in the sentences given white and non-white terrorists. The average sentences given these two groups differed by less than one year. Similarly, left- and right-wing terrorists, on average, received almost identical sentences (222 months and 224 months, respectively)."

In this section, a similar analysis is carried out on a larger sample covering a longer time period. Since prosecutorial discretion is so great, the analysis controls for what the terrorists did rather than for what they were charged with. For example, two members of the Symbionese Liberation Army, Bill and Emily Harris, were tried for kidnaping, because after a robbery they jumped into a car and drove away, taking the owner of the car hostage. Victor Gerena and the other Macheteros involved in the Hartford Wells Fargo robbery were charged with four separate counts of robbery, since the money belonged to four different banks.

In comparing the sentences handed out to different types of terrorists, four kinds of terrorist acts are distinguished. Those resulting in a fatality are considered separately from non-fatal incidents, while the non-fatal incidents are divided into three categories: bombings and arson, shootings, and robberies. Table 6.6 shows the average sentence received by different types of terrorists when a fatality resulted from the incident, while Table 6.7 compares the sentences handed down if no fatalities occurred.

Since courts are allowed to consider "uncharged and unconvicted conduct at sentencing," and the activities of the group as a whole, some variation between and within ideological categories is appropriate. For example, the higher than average sentences received by the

Table 6.6 Average sentence in incidents with fatality, by terrorist ideology (years)

Ideology	Sentence
Rightists	66.2
Anti-abortionists	50.0
Puerto Ricans	49.7
Black militants	37.0
Leftists	32.0
Cubans	30.0
White racists/Klan	17.0
Average, all cases	42.2

Table 6.7 Average sentence in incidents with no fatalities, by terrorist ideology (years)

Ideology	Bombing/ Arson	Shooting	Robbery
Puerto Ricans	46.1	16.0	16.0
Leftists	10.7	6.5	9.7
Rightists	9.5	3.0	25.0
Anti-abortionists	7.7	10.8	–
Cubans	7.0	–	–
White racists/Klan	2.8	0.0[a]	–
Jewish	2.7	2.2	–
Black militants	0.8	12.6	9.0
Average, all cases	11.6	11.6	15.3

Note
[a] Fines only.

Puerto Rican *independistas* for the Wells Fargo robbery were certainly affected by the fact that they were members of the Macheteros, a group that had gunned down American sailors in Puerto Rico. Indeed, the apparent harshness of the sentences imposed on almost all the Puerto Ricans presumably reflects the fact that they deliberately attacked both high-ranking members of the government and innocent civilians. The political climate – and the social attitudes of the judges – also seem to affect the treatment of some groups. Ten men found guilty of bombing sixteen black churches and homes in McComb were given suspended sentences by a Mississippi judge, who said that they had been "provoked" and were "young men starting out in life." Two white teenagers who gunned down a thirteen-year-old black boy in Birmingham AL were sentenced to seven months in prison, but released after a few days, and warned not to have another "lapse." The members and even the leaders of the Weather Underground were treated with remarkable leniency. Bernardine Dohrn was sentenced to probation and fined $1,500, with the judge turning down a prosecution request that she serve a nominal thirty days in jail because "she had suffered enough through her years in hiding separated from her family and friends." Cathlyn Platt Wilkerson, another leader, was freed after serving less than a year of her sentence – even though she had been convicted in connection with an explosion which killed three people. In this case, the judge thought that "no useful purpose would be served by her further imprisonment." Jeffrey Jones, whose apartment was described as a bomb factory, pleaded guilty to a charge of "manufacturing a bomb" and was placed on probation, and ordered to perform volunteer work in a day care center. A group of Weathermen who sniped at a police station in Cambridge MA were fined a total of $700. The treatment of members of the Jewish Defense League was also remarkable, given that they were responsible for at least three murders, and numerous bombings. Yet they were rarely prosecuted and received light sentences even when convicted. For example, one JDL member who bombed an Arab activist's home in 1972 was given three years' probation.

On the other hand, the treatment of anti-abortionist violence has tended to be extremely harsh. John Salvi, despite being obviously mentally ill, was sentenced to two life terms without parole for his part in the deaths of two abortion clinic receptionists.[15] Shannon Price, who fired a shot at an abortionist, was charged with attempted murder. Despite the fact that no one has ever been injured in any abortion clinic bombing, those convicted have received an average sentence of almost eight years, and many have received heavy fines in addition to their sentences. Fines, ranging from $1,500 to $357,073, were imposed in ten cases, with the average amount imposed being $158,983.

In only a handful of cases was the most extreme penalty handed down. In addition to Timothy McVeigh, nine other right-wing terrorists have been sentenced to die (although only two have actually been executed). The only other terrorists condemned to death were Oscar Collazo, the Puerto Rican nationalist who killed a guard outside President Truman's residence, Fred Evans, the leader of the Black Nation of New Libya, which was involved in a shoot-out in Cleveland, and Paul Hill, who murdered an abortionist.

Stepping over the line

Although vigorous law enforcement against terrorists is generally approved, certain methods are not considered legitimate in a democratic society. In some countries, death squads hunted down suspected terrorists and terrorist sympathizers, suspects were brutally interrogated or tortured, and legitimate activities by radical groups disrupted through "dirty tricks."

During the 1960s, the FBI developed the notorious Counterintelligence Program (COINTELPRO) against the Klan. At least 289 actions against white racist groups were carried out during the period, "most of them involving cheap psychological warfare and dirty tricks. . . . Agents leaned on Klansmen's employers, and a number of Klansmen lost their jobs" (Wade 1987). The FBI also tried to intimidate individual

Klansmen, and to provoke splits within the Klan organization. The murder of Vernon Dahmer by the KKK was solved after one of the Klansmen confessed and implicated himself and seven other Klansmen. According to one account, the confession was beaten out of him by a New York *mafioso*, Gregory Scarpa, who was brought in by the FBI.[16]

It has been noted that many of the tactics used against the Klan were also used against black militants a few years later (George and Wilcox 1992). Documents released under the Freedom of Information Act revealed that, through 1971, there were 295 FBI operations against black groups, including 233 against the Black Panthers.[17] The FBI fomented a war between the Black Panthers and Ron Karenga's US organization that led to several deadly shoot-outs between the two groups. In addition, undercover agents set the Panthers up by planting drugs and weapons in their homes and in BPP offices. In order to discredit the Panthers, the FBI forged and distributed thousands of copies of a "Black Panther Coloring Book," containing pictures of young black children attacking policemen with knives, "to the horror of many black leaders, who . . . began to dissociate themselves from the Panthers" (Volkman 1980: 156).

In Puerto Rico in the 1960s, on Hoover's orders, the FBI deliberately disrupted the activities of the nationalists. Hoover suggested "the use of informants to disrupt the movement and to create dissension within the groups . . . [and] the use of handwritten letters to plant the seeds of suspicion between various factions." As part of their campaign, agents sent anonymous letters containing sexual gossip about Juan Mari Bras, the leader of the Puerto Rican Independence Party, to party members (Fernandez 1987: 54). In the 1980s, it is alleged, a secret police unit, trained and armed by the FBI and the US Marshal's Office, carried out a series of political murders with the aim of destroying the independence movement. Three *independistas* vanished and are believed to have been killed by the "Defenders of Democracy." The group also bombed the offices of the Puerto Rican Bar Association, in an attempt to deter lawyers from defending *independistas*, and arrested nationalists on trumped-up charges and faked evidence.[18]

Measuring the effect of counterterrorist measures

Having described what has been done against terrorists, the impact of these measures will now be examined by studying three cases of terrorism; by black militants, by Puerto Rican *independistas*, and by the contemporary far right. Two outcome measures are used: the total number of terrorist incidents annually (except in the case of the black militants, where the six-month totals are used) and the total number of incidents, weighted according to severity. The severity of an incident is scored by adding the number killed or wounded. There are two general theories as to how law enforcement and the courts reduce crime, the attrition model and the punishment/deterrence model.

The attrition model. Most terrorist organizations are quite small. Hence if a significant number of terrorists are killed or captured, it is reasonable to assume that the organization will cease to exist, or at least that its activities will decline. The extent to which attrition takes its toll of the human capital of a group is estimated by calculating the cumulative total of those arrested and/or killed. The number of extremists arrested in each year is also coded. These may be overly simple measures of the impact of arrests, since not all terrorists are equally valuable to the group. Losing key personnel, such as leaders or skilled bomb makers, may have an especially severe impact on a group's ability to wage terrorism.

The punishment model. The rationale for punishing terrorist crimes severely is that it serves as a deterrent to others. As noted previously, terrorists do receive harsh sentences – usually greater than those meted out for comparable crimes committed by non-terrorists. The magnitude of punishment is calculated as the total years of sentences handed down to group members in each period. Since a death sentence sends an especially powerful message – and an execution an even stronger one – death sentences and executions are coded separately. It is arguable that the number of extremists killed by police serves not only as an aspect of personnel attrition, but also as a form of punishment – a pseudo-execution. The assumption is that the effect of all these punishments will be immediate – and will reduce terrorism in the same year or the following year.

The first step is to see whether there is any significant correlation between the law enforcement/criminal justice measures and the level of terrorist violence in the same year. The results are shown in Table 6.8. Only those correlations that are significant at the 0.05 level are given. The cumulative number arrested variable (and the cumulative number arrested and killed variable) are both significantly and negatively correlated with Puerto Rican terrorism.[19] In the case of both black terrorism and white racist terrorism, there is no correlation with cumulative arrests, but there is a very high correlation with the number of arrests. Total sentence years and death sentences are both linked with fluctuations in white racist terrorism. As regards black terrorism, the number of militants killed by police is positively correlated with the number and severity of terrorist incidents.

Table 6.8 Same-year correlations between terrorist countermeasures and terrorist incidents

Type of terrorist	Incidents	Weighted incidents
Puerto Ricans		
Arrests	–	–
Sentences	–	–
Cumulative arrests	−0.482	−0.465
Blacks		
Arrests	+0.630	+0.928
Sentences	–	–
Killed by police	+0.642	+0.655
Cumulative arrests	–	–
White racists		
Arrests	–	+0.505
Sentences	–	+0.767
Killed by police	–	–
Death sentences	–	+0.522
Cumulative arrests	–	–

Note
Correlations shown only if significant at >0.05 level.

These results can be interpreted as follows. The Puerto Rican case serves as a good illustration of the attrition model. A high-ranking FBI official (Monroe 1982: 146) noted that "one of the reasons for the FALN's relative inactivity [since 1980] was the arrest and conviction of several of their members." Similarly, Hoffman (1986: 4) attributed the sharp decline in Puerto Rican terrorism in 1985 to "the continuing success achieved by the FBI as well as local law enforcement agencies in tracking down and arresting wanted and suspected terrorists." The correlation between cumulative arrests and Puerto Rican terrorism shown in Table 6.8 provides statistical support for these judgements. (See also Figure 6.1 for a graphic illustration of the association between the two variables.) The FALN is estimated to have had about fifty members and the Macheteros probably had about the same number. Thus by the mid-1980s both groups had lost a considerable proportion of their strength. The impact of the arrests was heightened by the fact that those arrested included two of the leaders (Torres and Lopez) and William Morales, the FALN's most expert bomb maker.[20]

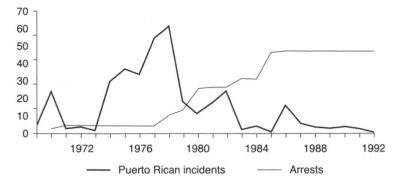

Figure 6.1 Arrests of Puerto Rican terrorists and the decline of Puerto Rican terrorism, 1969–92

A very different pattern is seen in the other two cases. The strong same-year correlations between the terrorist activity and law enforcement/criminal justice measures seen for both black and white racists is most easily explained as a response by the authorities. When there is a lot of terrorist activity, police arrest more terrorists, and the courts punish them more severely. In the case of the black militants, whose primary target was the police, the fact that more of them were killed by police during periods of increased terrorist activity is exactly what would be expected. This interpretation is supported by another fact. The Oklahoma City bombing was the worst terrorist atrocity to occur on American soil prior to September 11, and as anticipated we find a statistically significant increase in arrests of, and sentences imposed on, white racist terrorists after that date. Specifically the average annual number of arrests prior to the Oklahoma bombing was twelve compared with twenty for the years following the bombing. Similarly the average number of sentence years handed down prior to the bombing were lower than in the years following (an annual average of 137 sentence years compared with 381 sentence years).[21]

However, from a law enforcement/criminal justice point of view, the important question is whether these arrests and punishments *subsequently* reduced the level of violence? To find out, the variables were lagged for one year. However, no significant decline was observed in either white racist or black terrorism in the year after the arrests and punishments (which is consistent with the previously noted lack of any relationship between cumulative arrests and the level of violence). Indeed, the death sentences imposed on white racists were followed by higher levels of violence. Why is this? Why did not black terrorism and white racist terrorism decline after large numbers of terrorists were arrested, as happened with Puerto Rican terrorism? The answer lies in the fact that the terrorism was different and so were the arrests.

Unlike the Puerto Rican case, where terrorist *organizations* were responsible for planned campaigns, black terrorism – for the most part – was carried out by the violent fringe of an extremist movement. Although there were some organized terrorist groups such as the Black Liberation Army, the Black Panther Party *per se* was not a terrorist organization, even though some of its members engaged in terrorist acts. Black terrorism was a largely unorganized – almost spontaneous – activity carried out by unskilled amateurs. Furthermore, since the Black Panthers were arrested indiscriminately for minor offences, it could not be expected that the arrests would have much effect.

The current wave of white racist terrorism seems to be even more amorphous. As with the black militants, we are dealing with an extremist movement that has a violent terrorist fringe. The concept of "leaderless resistance" has been adopted by many right-wing extremists, so that several recent deadly attacks have been carried out by lone terrorists, who have only the most tenuous links with any extremist organization. Timothy McVeigh is one notorious example, but several others come to mind. Right-wing extremists have not been harassed in the same way that militant black groups were. However, as pointed out earlier, large numbers have been arrested for merely talking about engaging in terrorism. It is unlikely that such arrests will reduce or prevent terrorism.[22]

Indeed, indiscriminate repression of extremist groups and individuals holding extremist opinions can be not merely ineffective but counterproductive. Terrorism is usually linked with a wider social movement, and the most valuable resource a terrorist group has is its ability to mobilize social support. To modify the Maoist slogan slightly, "a successful terrorist must swim like a fish in a sea of popular support." All successful terrorist campaigns depend on such popular support. The FALN and the Macheteros were vulnerable because they had only a small degree of support within the Puerto Rican community. On the other hand black militants had a high degree of support, and the support for contemporary right-wing extremists is not trivial.

People are often attracted to extremist movements because of what they perceive as brutality and injustice by the authorities. In Puerto Rico, the murder of two terrorists by police (the Cerro Maravilla affair) became a major issue in the 1984 elections and increased support for the *independistas*. After the trial and imprisonment of Huey Newton for the murder of a policeman, the Panthers launched a "Free Huey" campaign. "Panther chapters were formed in a score of cities and the membership surged to perhaps two thousand" (Goodell 1973: 115). One reason why contemporary anti-government groups are able to recruit a substantial membership is that many people believe that the government has committed violent acts against its own citizens. A large number of Americans believe that, at Waco, the FBI set fire to the Branch Davidians' compound, or shot at the Davidians when they were trying to escape the fire. A majority believe that the FBI lied about what happened at Waco (Boyer 1999). According to most accounts, the Oklahoma City bombing by Timothy McVeigh was an act of revenge for what happened at Waco.[23] It is important to remember that many terrorist acts are intended to send a message and to change public opinion. Law enforcement efforts to reduce terrorism must be carefully crafted to avoid increasing the alienation and hostility that many Americans currently feel towards the government.

Notes

1 For an account of the Meridian affair see Nelson (1993). Nelson (1993: 234) concludes that "at best the tactics had the earmarks of entrapping the Klan members . . . the worst-case interpretation of the evidence was that the plan involved a death trap."

2 Epstein examines the circumstances surrounding the deaths of twenty-eight Panthers, and concludes that there are no grounds for claiming, as many liberals did, that a pattern of police genocide existed.

3 In December 1999, Governor Pedro Rossello publicly apologized to the victims of state spying and offered $6,000 to those whose *carpetas* exceeded fifty pages. In May 2000, the FBI acknowledged its involvement and released its surveillance files to House Representative Jose Serrano (Marino 1999).

4 I considered arrests for marijuana possession as harassment. The high number of Panthers arrested for drugs or regular street crimes is indicative of their lumpenproletariat social background.

5 Predictably, this brought charges that the police had violated their civil rights, and a judge issued an injunction against such police tactics ("Fear in the streets of San Francisco" 1974).

6 Flynn and Gerhardt (1989: 44, 67, 213) describe how FBI agents talked to his employer in an attempt to have Robert Mathews fired, and how police stopped David Lane and confiscated leaflets from him. "They had broken no law but police like to let radicals know that they are being watched."

7 The incident had some strange features. According to the victim, after driving past the compound, she doubled back towards the entrance after her son had accidentally dropped his wallet out of the car window – then her car backfired. This was mistaken for gunfire and they were pursued and assaulted by the security guards (Claiborne 2000).

8 The SPLC is not the only group bringing civil suits against hate crimes. The Center for Constitutional Rights won a $535,000 judgement in 1982 against the Justice Knights of the Klan on behalf of five black women injured during a shooting incident in Chattanooga. The center is currently bringing a suit against the World Church of the Creator after Benjamin Smith, an ex-member of the group, went on a shooting spree that left two dead and nine wounded.

9 Columnist Jack Anderson claimed that the clean-cut FBI agents could not infiltrate the student subculture of "beards, beads, and bell bottoms," but Jeffers (1972: 189) argues that the problem was the lack of informants willing to trade information for cash.

10 As Daley (1973: 85) points out, this is true of crime in general. "Detective novels were one thing, real-life crime solving was something else. Crimes were solved by informants, not deduction."

11 Details on the use of informants are understandably hard to come by, but interesting accounts can be found in Volkman (1980), Anthony (1990), Rosenthal (2000), and "Undercover Policeman" (1965: A1).

12 Rowe was riding in the car with the Klansmen who shot and killed Mrs Liuzzo. The federal government was later sued by her children for not controlling Rowe's violent activities.

13 According to Zimroth (1974: 49), the FBI had comparatively poor intelligence about the Panthers, and relied primarily upon paid informants, some of whom were very unreliable, and on local police departments. Attorney General Ramsey Clark estimated that during his tenure about 90 percent of the FBI's intelligence about black militants came from local police departments.

14 Since our focus is on the contemporary impact of law enforcement, this does not include cases in which terrorists were captured or convicted long after their terrorist acts. Thus the recent trials of Kathleen Soliah of the SLA, Sam Bowers of the KKK, and Byron de la Beckwith (murderer of Medger Evers) for crimes committed in the 1960s and 1970s are ignored.

15 At his trial, it was reported that Salvi had delusions of a Masonic conspiracy against Catholics, and wanted the Vatican to issue its own currency. He committed suicide in prison, where he was reportedly "disheveled and babbling," and was denied medication for his condition (*Washington Post* November 30, 1996).

16 Scarpa, who was an informant for the FBI, and an FBI agent kidnaped the Klansman, Lawrence Byrd, drove him to a nearby military base, where Scarpa beat a confession out of him. "Lawrence was a tough guy – a big raw-boned country boy – but he was beat up so bad he was never the same after that" (Dannen 1996: 71).

17 According to Volkman (1980: 156), the bureau spent $7.4 million on informants in their war against the Black Panthers, a sum twice what they spent to obtain information on organized crime.

18 The information on the Defenders of Democracy was uncovered by a Puerto Rican Senate investigation (Weiner 1992).

19 Since the two variables are highly correlated with each other, and since the cumulative arrest variable is a better predictor, it is the only one shown in Table 6.8.

20 Fernandez (1987: 234–5) suggests a different explanation. Violence declined not because the Macheteros were "demoralized, fatally weakened, or frightened" but because they were concerned that further attacks would "adversely affect the plight of their imprisoned comrades." However, if this were true, one would anticipate that after harsh sentences were handed down, there would have been a resumption of violence – which did not occur.

21 In order to compare average number of arrests and years sentenced before versus after the Oklahoma City bombing, independent t tests were calculated: t/arrests (19) $= -1.755$, $p < 0.10$; t/sentence years (19) $= -1.795$, $p < 1.0$.

22 For example, of the twelve members of the Arizona Viper militia who were arrested, half were released on bond as posing no threat to society, and most charges against several defendants were dropped three months later (Suro 1998).

23 McVeigh had visited Waco during the siege, and apparently believed that the assault had been ordered from the ATF offices in the Murrah Federal Building (Jones 1998: 57).

7 Impacts and consequences

If terrorism is important, it is because it has certain consequences and impacts. This chapter examines these under five headings: the economic costs of terrorism; changes in social behavior and public opinion; how the media portray terrorism; terrorism as a political issue; counterterrorism policies and the outcomes of terrorism. The September 11 events were compared to the attack on Pearl Harbor, and in many respects the scale of the attack dwarfs all previous acts of terrorism in the United States – or indeed in the world.[1] If we consider the loss of life as a measure of the severity of terrorism, this single attack took more lives than all the terrorist attacks in America over the previous half-century. Therefore, in examining the effects of terrorism, the results of September 11 will be considered separately.

The economic costs of terrorism

Prior to September 11 the economic costs of terrorism within the United States were relatively trivial. Terrorist bombings occasionally caused costly property damage. The explosion at the Army Math Center in 1970 resulted in damage of over $2.5 million (about $10 million at current prices), while damage from the World Trade Center bombing of 1993 was estimated at $250 million (more than $400 million at current prices). An audit conducted for the state of Oklahoma concluded that the cost of the damage resulting from the Oklahoma City bombing totaled at least $652 million. Terrorist robberies and other forms of "self-financing" have sometimes netted large sums, with more than $1 million being stolen in three cases. In 1981, the M19CO got $1.6 million when they robbed a Brinks truck, and in 1984 the Order got $3.6 million in the robbery of another Brinks truck. The record was set by the Puerto Rican Macheteros, who stole $7.1 million from a Wells Fargo depot in 1983.

Most bombings, however, caused only minor damage, and most robberies were of modest amounts.[2] Certainly, of all such crimes, those committed for ideological reasons constitute an insignificant proportion. For the last five years for which statistics are available, the Bureau of Alcohol, Tobacco and Firearms recorded 10,321 bombings, of which terrorist bombings numbered only thirty-seven, or 0.4 percent. Over the twenty years 1980–2000 terrorist robberies accounted for only 0.2 percent of all bank robberies, with the total stolen about $20 million.[3]

The direct costs of the September 11 attack were certainly not trivial, and the indirect economic effects were even more significant. The property damage losses may run as high as $50 billion, while the life insurance industry anticipates paying out as much as $5 billion to the families of those killed. More important are the changing perceptions of risk by businesses and the public. The sheer unpredictability of terrorist attacks makes it difficult to plan for them. Such low-probability but high-consequence events are either disregarded or exaggerated. After September 11 the insurance industry warned that premiums on buildings near nuclear plants and in other high-risk areas might triple, and that they would not cover losses from terrorism unless the government provided them with financial guarantees.[4] The perceived (and probably exaggerated) risk of terrorism leads to higher insurance costs, increasing prices to consumers and reducing profits to firms. Increased security, whether it involves buying metal detectors or hiring extra guards, also results in higher prices and lower profits (Pearlstein 2001). The long-term effects of terrorism on consumer psychology are still unknown, but people are concerned about their personal safety, reluctant to travel, and cutting back on major purchases. Movie attendance is down, restaurants report fewer customers, and airline passenger numbers fell from 9 million per week before September 11 to 7.5 million at the end of November. Although the economy was already weakening, the attacks certainly worsened the situation. The jobless rate jumped from 4.9 percent in September to 5.4 percent in October – the largest monthly increase in two decades.

Changes in social behavior and public opinion resulting from terrorism

In some places, such as Northern Ireland, or the Basque provinces of Spain, terrorism produced drastic changes in public life styles. People were afraid to go out to restaurants, cinemas, and social events. The use of public transport declined. Tourism dried to a trickle, and people moved away from dangerous areas or emigrated. Certain groups, such as politicians, journalists, and other elite individuals, were especially affected. For many prominent Germans life in the 1970s – when the Red Army Faction was active – resembled a state of siege. In Uruguay as a result of the threat from the Tupamaros, the elite were forced into "living almost an underground life . . . restricting their movements, being constantly protected by bodyguards even in their own homes" (Porzekanski 1973: 46–7). Nothing like this occurred in the United States, presumably because terrorism – until recently – posed only a minor threat.[5]

Where terrorism did take place, even those who witnessed the incident were apparently unaffected. For example, in October 1977, there was an explosion outside the New York Public Library on Fifth Avenue. The bomb, set by the FALN, was loud enough to be heard a block away in the *New Yorker* office, and a reporter from the magazine rushed to the scene. His account ("Blast" 1977) is interesting for what it reveals about the *lack* of public reaction. Although the bomb squad quickly appeared and began searching for undetonated explosives, "business was being carried on pretty much as usual inside the building" and he emphasizes how library patrons were "unruffled." One commented that he had come from Idaho to examine a manuscript, "and I'm not about to let a lousy little bombing stop me." The article notes that the bombing didn't make the front page of any of the major New York papers. The bombing of the Olympic Park in Atlanta killed one woman and injured hundreds, but the very next day fans lined up defiantly and attendance was reportedly unaffected.

In only a very few instances did terrorism result in more than trivial short-lived effects, and in all these cases the violence continued for several months or even years. For example, clashes between rival groups spread "fear and grief through black Islamic communities across the US" in the early 1970s ("Religious split among blacks" 1973). In San Francisco a series of killings of whites by the Death Angels (a black racist group) over a six-month period in 1973–4 crippled the city's night life, and business suffered a drastic decline, with "shopping-area parking lots less than half filled" (Howard 1979: 347). In the early 1970s, fear gripped the black community when a lone white racist stalked the ghetto neighborhoods of Dayton, shooting down over a score of victims. Black leaders asked the city to declare a state of emergency, and citizens' patrols were organized (Vasconez 1999).[6] In Miami, chronic violence by Cuban terrorists led to an unusual interest in security. "Even modest householders had detailed information about perimeter defenses, areas of containment, motion monitors, and closed circuit television surveillance." Booby-trap bombs had become "commonplace enough in Miami during the 1970s to create a market for devices designed to flick the ignition in a parked car by remote signal" (Didion 1987: 25, 100).

The September 11 attacks generated widespread fear throughout the country, not just in the areas where the planes crashed. One study found that nine out of ten adults showed clinical signs of stress, half of them reporting symptoms of major stress such as insomnia. More than a third of children reported having nightmares (Schuster 2001). New prescriptions for tranquillizers such as Xanax and Valium rose sharply, especially in New York City and Washington DC, in the weeks following the attacks. Psychiatric hot lines also recorded a significant increase in the number of callers, although the number had begun to taper off by mid-October (Okie 2001). This trend, which parallels the results of several surveys on anxiety and stress, suggests that public fears will gradually decline if there is no new major terrorist attack.[7] If the public become less fearful, then presumably there will be no major permanent disruption of American life styles.

This was certainly the case after the Oklahoma City bombing, as the analysis by Lewis (2000) of national survey data in the 1990s shows. Lewis notes that while terrorism *in the abstract* was seen as an important problem, the public did not perceive terrorism as posing any *personal* threat. Although after the Oklahoma City bombing the proportion rating terrorism an important issue increased from 63 percent to 89 percent, the concern had subsided considerably by the summer of 1996. Furthermore even immediately after the Oklahoma City bombing, a majority (57 percent) were "not too worried" or "not worried at all" that they or a relative would become a victim of a terrorist attack. In another survey, almost three-quarters of those polled said that they did not plan to change their "personal life or routine in order to reduce the chance of becoming a victim of terrorism." Lewis concludes that the public had a "realistic assessment [of the dangers of terrorism] despite political and media hyperbole," hence their "temperate response." The public think that terrorism is "likely to happen – but to someone else."

Lewis's assessment holds up even after the September 11 attack. Table 7.1 shows public concern about terrorism, as measured by the percentage who said they were "very" or "somewhat" worried that they or someone in their family would become a victim of a terrorist attack. The question was first asked in April 1995, immediately after the Oklahoma City bombing, and asked irregularly after that date

Table 7.1 "Very or somewhat worried that they or someone in their family will be a victim of a terrorist attack" (%)

April 1995	42 (Oklahoma City bombing)
April 1996	35
July 1996	39
Aug 1996[a]	29
April 1997[a]	36
June 1997[a]	21
August 1998	32
April 2000	24
September 11, 2001	58 (World Trade Center/Pentagon attack)
September 14–15, 2001	51
September 21–2, 2001	49
October 5–6, 2001	59 (anthrax letters scare)
October 11–14, 2001	51
October 19–21, 2001	43
November 2–4, 2001	40

Sources: [a] Lewis (2000). All others from Gallup reports.

until September 11, since when it has been asked almost every other week. The last survey shown is for November 2001. If public concern is looked at in relation to major terrorist events, it appears that public anxiety increases after each attack, but then dissipates fairly quickly. In fact if the period after September 11 is considered (when public opinion was surveyed almost weekly) it can be seen that public concern declines sharply within a matter of days.

Media coverage

The media play an important role in the formation of public opinion, since they control the flow of information to the public. They can emphasize or ignore an issue, and can also define the nature of the problem raised by terrorism. On the other hand it is often argued that terrorists use and exploit the media to gain publicity. One definition of terrorism sees it as "theater," aimed at an audience, and intended to produce changes in public opinion and the political situation. Schmid and de Graf (1982) argue that terrorism is sometimes an attempt at communication, aimed at drawing attention to the terrorists' cause. As an indication of the ability of terrorists to draw attention to themselves, let us consider media coverage of domestic terrorism, using the *Reader's Guide to Periodical Literature* as a source. The annual number of articles on domestic terrorism provides a somewhat

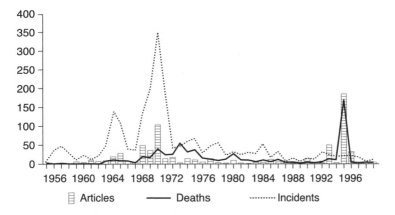

Figure 7.1 Media coverage of terrorism compared with the number of deaths and incidents, 1955–99

crude measure of attention, and Figure 7.1 shows how media coverage has fluctuated over time, and in relation to the number of terrorist incidents and fatalities. Spectacular events such as the World Trade Center bombing of 1993 or the Oklahoma City bombing of 1995 obviously attract media attention. Coverage was also high during the late 1960s when leftists and black militants were most active.

Certain kinds of terrorism have received more attention than would appear warranted if we consider the coverage in relation to the number of deaths that have resulted. Coincidentally, the total number of articles on domestic terrorism (699) is almost the same as the number of fatalities (661) before September 11, so Figure 7.2 shows the two totals for each ideological category of terrorism. Since the Oklahoma City bombing is in a class of its own, in terms of both the number of victims (168) and media attention (169 articles), it is shown separately. The greatest discrepancy in coverage concerns leftist terrorism, where the number of articles greatly exceeds the number of deaths, although this can be explained by the fact that leftists were responsible for a high proportion of terrorist incidents even if few resulted in fatalities. Other "overreported" categories include anti-abortionist and Klan terrorism, while Cuban terrorism and Puerto Rican terrorism are relatively "underreported." There is more coverage of Islamic terrorism than would be expected, given the number of deaths resulting from it prior to the September 11 attacks, perhaps indicating a degree of foresight by the media.

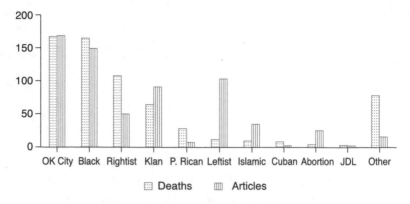

Figure 7.2 Media coverage of terrorism compared with the number of deaths from terrorism, by ideology

In terms of content, the coverage of political violence by the national media is almost invariably negative. A study by Picard and Adams (1987) of how terrorism was characterized in the *New York Times*, *Washington Post*, and *Los Angeles Times*, for the years 1980–85, found that the most common terms used to describe terrorist acts were "despicable," "brutal," and "criminal," while the perpetrators were most commonly described as "murderers," "criminals," and "cowards." In so far as terrorism is intended to attract sympathetic attention to a political cause, it must be deemed a failure. Paletz *et al.* (1982) analyzed the *New York Times*'s coverage of the Irish Republican Army, the Italian Red Brigades, and the Puerto Rican FALN from 1977 to 1979. They concluded that terrorist motives and goals were largely ignored, that official perspectives were reinforced, and that government repression was legitimated. Gerbner (1991) argued that media coverage of terrorism emphasized the dangers that it posed, thereby mobilizing "support for repression, often on a higher scale than warranted by the threat."

Despite this generally negative treatment, there are some differences in the coverage of different groups by the media. Paletz *et al.* (1982) found that the IRA position was often "presented eloquently by sympathizers," whereas the FALN was described as a group of "fanatics" who wanted to make Puerto Rico independent "whether Puerto Rico likes it or not." (Presumably this is partly due to the fact that Puerto Rican terrorism was directed against the United States, whereas IRA terrorism was directed against Britain.) The white racists and the anti-abortionists are portrayed in an especially negative fashion. The dangers that they pose are exaggerated; their victims are personalized and remembered. Political and civic leaders are quoted frequently, condemning them in the strongest terms. The coverage of anti-abortion violence sometimes verges on hysteria. Following the banning of the web site the "Nuremberg Files," which listed the names of doctors who performed abortions, the *Washington Post* published two op-ed articles by Suzanna Sherry and Amitai Etzioni. Sherry (1999) claimed that the doctors were "so afraid that they told their children to hide in the bathtub if they heard gunfire" and that it was "intolerable that doctors who perform abortions must fear for their lives and the lives of their families." Etzioni (1999) described the web site as "encouraging the killings of physicians and their children." In fact no attacks were made against the children/families of abortionists, and in only one case, that of Barnett Slepian in October 1998, was a doctor attacked at his home. With leftist and black terrorism the coverage is more mixed. Although their actions are condemned, their viewpoints are described – sometimes even sympathetically.[8] Although their critics are quoted, so are their supporters.[9]

Media coverage of Islamic terrorism, both before and after September 11, has generally ignored the motives of those responsible. During the trial of the 1993 bombers, the writer of a *Newsweek* article ("A terrorist plot without a story") was puzzled by the lack of "a coherent reason for bombing the World Trade Center . . . the best we have are vague references to US support for Israel" (Morgenthau 1994: 28). Rather than publish Osama bin Laden's statements in which he explains in detail the rationale for his *jihad*, the media offer psychobabble about fundamentalist fears of the modern world, and dismiss his followers as "madmen" or "evil fanatics." Following the September 11 attacks, both newspaper and television coverage exaggerated the dangers of nuclear terrorism and bioterrorism. Not unexpectedly, one study found that "extensive television viewing was associated with a substantial stress reaction" (Schuster 2001). The media were also criticized for providing information that could be of value to potential terrorists, such as how to disseminate anthrax spores, and details of the vulnerabilities of US suspension bridges.[10]

Terrorism as a political issue

Terrorism can be said to be a political issue when politicians begin to make statements about it, and a *national* political issue when Presidents make statements about it.[11] However, the willingness of politicians to speak out is affected by who the victims are. President Johnson was reluctant to deal with Klan terrorism in the south until three civil rights workers were killed, two of them white. Only then did he unleash the FBI against the Klan, and order the military to search for the missing men. As the widow of one of the murdered men declared, "We all know that this search with hundreds of sailors is because Andrew Goodman and my husband are white. If only Chaney was involved, nothing would have been done."[12] Despite considerable pressure from the National Organization of Women and other feminist groups, President Reagan remained silent about attacks on abortion clinics until early 1985. Following a series of bombings in Pensacola FL, he finally spoke out: "I will do all in my power to assure that the guilty are brought to justice," he said. "I condemn in the strongest terms those individuals who perpetrate these and all such violent anarchist activities" (Magnusson 1985).

Usually, however, major acts of terrorism are quickly denounced by politicians. After the assassination of the Rev. Martin Luther King, President Lyndon Johnson expressed shock and sorrow at "the brutal slaying," and proclaimed a national day of mourning for the civil rights leader. Following the bombing of the Army Math Research Center at the University of Wisconsin, President Nixon condemned the "cancerous disease of terrorism," and argued that "What corrodes a society even more deeply than violence itself is the acceptance of violence, the condoning of terror, the excusing of inhuman acts" (Bates 1992: 51). President Clinton frequently spoke out against terrorism. Within hours of the Oklahoma City blast, he vowed that the country would not tolerate terrorism and that he would "not allow the people of this country to be intimidated by evil cowards." Clinton called the bombing of the Olympic Park in Atlanta "an evil act of terror. . . . aimed at innocent people . . . an act of cowardice." During a visit to Denver in 1997, he denounced two racial murders committed by skinheads as "vicious, violent crimes." The 1995 shooting deaths at two abortion clinics in suburban Boston MA were deplored as "meaningless violence" by Clinton, and the 1998 murder of abortionist Dr Barnett Slepian was a "brutal and tragic act."

Politicians act as well as talk. They get tough on terrorism. Laws are passed creating new offenses, and giving police and judges new powers. More money is allocated to the security budget. After each of the three main atrocities in the last decade, the 1993 World Trade Center bombing, the 1995 Oklahoma City bombing, and September 11, there was a flurry of political activity. In 1996, Congress passed and President Clinton signed the Antiterrorism Bill, which granted the federal government new powers to deny entry to suspected terrorists, to deport aliens suspected of having terrorist ties, and to prosecute those who raised funds for terrorist groups. The Clinton administration had proposed expanded wiretapping powers, and a military role in domestic terrorism cases involving biological and chemical weapons and the tagging of materials that might be used to build an explosive device, but these proposals were dropped. An extra billion dollars was allocated to law enforcement agencies, and the guidelines for FBI action were relaxed (Heymann 1998). The FBI hired hundreds of new agents and, with this increased manpower, has increased its investigation of domestic terrorism since the Oklahoma City bombing from about 100 cases to over 900 (Lewis 2000).

In the aftermath of September 11 unprecedented new emergency powers were granted to the government. The USA Patriot Act, as the anti-terrorism legislation is titled, allows the FBI and intelligence agencies to share grand jury and wiretap information, increases the penalties for committing terrorist acts or sheltering or funding terrorists, makes an act of terrorism against a mass transit system a federal crime, gives the Attorney General the power to detain non-citizens without charge, allows federal agents to use "roving wiretaps" whereby they can tap any phone that a suspect uses, and grants federal agents new powers of surveillance over internet and e-mail communications. The Act created the foundation for a domestic intelligence-gathering system on a scale never before seen in the United States, and both conservatives and liberals criticized the bill as a threat to civil liberties. Civil libertarians were also concerned about the Attorney General's decision to monitor conversations between lawyers and suspected terrorists, and the FBI's questioning of thousands of foreign students and visitors from the Middle East. By an executive order President Bush created an Office of Homeland Security, and appointed Tom Ridge as director with the task of developing a national strategy and coordinating the domestic response to the terrorism threat. Later another executive order empowered the President to order military trials for international terrorists and their collaborators. Congress voted to increase spending on intelligence gathering by $1 billion over the previous year, although not all of this is directed against terrorism (Pincus 2001). After the anthrax scare, the Senate introduced legislation providing an additional $3.2 billion to deal with the threat from bioterrorism.

Funding has increased from $4 billion in 1990 to $9.6 in 2001, and, adjusted for inflation, approximately $70 billion of federal money was spent on counterterrorism between 1990 and 2001, with a further $14.5 billion already budgeted for 2002. Figure 7.3, which shows the

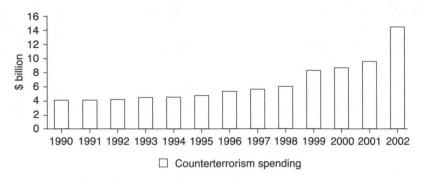

Figure 7.3 Counterterrorism spending, 1990–2002

growth since 1990, provides an indicator of the growth of counter-terrorism as a political issue.[13]

Counterterrorism policies and the outcomes of terrorism

Finally it should be noted that, in terms of the goals and strategies of the terrorists themselves, terrorism has almost always been a failure.[14] Legally enforced racial segregation is no more. There is no separate black nation. No socialist revolution has occurred. Puerto Rico is still a US possession. More than a million abortions were carried out last year. In fact, terrorism is often counterproductive. As an editorial in a leftist publication asked bitterly of the Symbionese Liberation Army's campaign: "What have been the political effects of the Hearst kidnaping? It has created more public sympathy across class lines for the Hearst family than it has been able to muster for half a century. . . . It has created a pretext for repressive police actions against revolutionary, prison and welfare groups" ("Terrorism and the left" 1974: 21). After the Math Research Center bombing there was "a general retreat from violence, not only locally, but across the country." The writer James Michener claimed that the revulsion following the incident was the watershed, marking the end of revolutionary youth violence (Bates 1992: 443).

Terrorism by right-wing extremists has backfired on several occasions. In Billings, Montana racist vandalism was met with community outrage. After two Jewish homes decorated with Hanukkah menorahs were attacked, "Christian churches distributed photocopies of menorahs. . . . Within days, the nine-candled symbol was displayed in thousands of windows across the city" ("Montana outrage stalls skinheads" 1994). In Texas, the gruesome murder of James Byrd by three white racists – he was dragged to death behind a pickup truck – led to "greater empathy and understanding between whites and blacks [within his home town], a deeper harmony achieved through community meetings, church sermons and discussions, personal introspection and honest conversations" (Duggan 1999).

Not only did terrorism fail to achieve the goals of the terrorists, but most waves of terrorism were short-lived. Why is this? Ross and Gurr (1989) suggest four conditions that lead to the decline of political terrorism, which they call pre-emption, deterrence, backlash, and burnout. Pre-emption and deterrence largely overlap since they refer to counterterrorist policies, and it is often difficult to distinguish between the two. Killings and imprisonment of terrorists are cited as examples of pre-emption, but are usually justified as having a deterrent function. Their claim, that the "loss of political capabilities probably contributes more to the decline of terrorist campaigns in democratic societies than any actions taken by the authorities," may be true of the revolutionary leftists, but this is the exception, not the rule. Almost all the terrorist campaigns in the United States stopped because a significant proportion of their members were eventually caught or killed by the police. Often vigorous law enforcement was combined with repression of sympathizers and supporters. The effect of "backlash," the loss of political support for the terrorists' acts and objectives, was rarely the immediate cause of any group's demise. However, groups which have more popular support may be able to avoid capture and find new recruits and hence last longer than groups with less support.

Notes

1 The Oklahoma City bombing with 168 fatalities was the worst attack before September 11. Hoffman (1998) argues that terrorist attacks have become more deadly, as terrorists escalate their attacks in order to achieve an impact on public opinion.
2 One exception to this may be the attacks on abortion clinics. For 109 incidents in which the cost of the damage is given, the average is $94,450.
3 In estimating the proportion of terrorist robberies as a percentage of all bank robberies, and the total value stolen in terrorist robberies, I used the figure of 368 terrorist robberies cited by Mizell (1998: 12). For most robberies, the amount stolen is not given, and in these cases it was assumed that the average value taken was the same as the average for all bank robberies ($4,802), according to the most recent *Statistical Yearbook*.
4 Insurers want a government-backed pool, while the Bush administration proposes that the government would pay for most terrorism-related

claims in 2002, but that its responsibility would be reduced over the next three years.

5 One 1978 story was about increased security precautions by a "wealthy business executive" but emphasized how unusual this was. "In a city like Rome, there would be nothing unusual about such precautions. But this executive lives in Los Angeles" ("Is the US next?").

6 The same kind of widespread public fear and changes in behavior are produced by serial killers (Fisher 1997).

7 Okie (2001) cites polls taken by the Pew Research Center for the People and the Press a few days after the attacks and three weeks later. The proportion saying that they were depressed fell from 71 percent to 42 percent, while the proportion suffering from insomnia had dropped from 33 percent to 18 percent.

8 Several articles portrayed the Black Panthers as victims of police repression. See "Open season on Panthers?" (1969), "Out to get the Panthers" (1969), "Persecution and assassination of the Black Panther Party" (1969). Anti-war radicals were portrayed sympathetically in "FBI's toughest foe: the kids" (1970).

9 Cuban terrorism is an example of sympathetic treatment by the local if not the national media. One Cuban *émigré* claimed that "Serious responsibility for the persistence of terrorism in Miami falls on the city's communication media, especially on the exile press, which has tended to glorify the terrorists" ("Cuban exiles: Miami, haven for terror" 1977).

10 One letter to the *Washington Post* ("Tipsheet for terrorists" November 10, 2001) accused the paper of being a "how to" manual for terrorists.

11 When Presidents speak out, so do other politicians. For example, after the murder of Barnett Slepian both Governor Pataki and Senator D'Amato called for the death penalty for his killer. After John Salvi killed two receptionists at abortion clinics outside Boston MA, Governor Weld declared, "This man is nothing more than a terrorist. No one is going to settle moral arguments by violence."

12 During the 1964 election campaign, Johnson condemned "the use of violence and terror by clandestine hate groups," and tried to embarrass Goldwater by noting that some Klan leaders had expressed support for the Republican candidate.

13 Sources for Figure 7.3 include the Annual Report to Congress on Combating Terrorism, published by the Office of Management and Budget, which identifies the counterterrorism budget of each federal agency, and Lewis (2000). For the years since 1998, the figures are from the Henry L. Stimson Center. The estimated budget for 2002 includes the additional funds voted by the Senate against bioterrorism and the extra $1 billion budgeted for intelligence gathering.

14 The sole exception was terrorism by the Jewish Defense League. According to Friedman (1990: 5), "JDL violence forced the American Jewish establishment and, in turn, the US government to make the free immigration of Soviet Jews a top priority."

8 The future of American terrorism

In this final chapter, some predictions will be made concerning the threat of terrorism on American soil over the next decade or so. Such an analysis requires answering three questions. Who are the dangerous groups? What are the goals of these dangerous groups? What resources and capabilities do these groups have?

There is general agreement that two groups, Islamic and rightist extremists, are likely to engage in terrorist acts within America, although different experts have placed more or less emphasis on one or the other at different times. In 1996, the FBI declared that Islamic radicals represented the greatest threat. While their base of support lies overseas, in the Muslim world, as John O'Neill, the head of the FBI's counterterrorism section, noted, they "now have the capability and the support infrastructure in the United States to attack us here if they choose." O'Neill added that there was also a growing danger from "the anti-government movement, particularly the militias. . . . We are seeing a threat from international groups and the domestic groups at the same time" (quoted in Rowan 1996: 13). Two years later, after the Oklahoma City bombing, a *US News and World Report* article focused on the danger from the right, noting that "two years after Oklahoma City, violent sects still abound." The article concluded, "A serious terrorism threat also remains from international groups, particularly from the Mideast. Yet while international terrorists have repeatedly attacked American targets overseas, they have not struck inside the United States since 1993" (Kaplan and Tharp 1998). Morris Dees and Mark Potok (2001), writing on the eve of Timothy McVeigh's execution, claimed that while support for the militia movement had dwindled, there was still a significant threat from revolutionary neo-Nazi hate groups. Writing days after the destruction of the Twin Towers, Vincent Cannistraro (2001), former head of CIA counterterrorism operations, saw both al Qaeda and Christian Identity as posing a "virulent threat." Experts can be wrong, but it is clear that both Islamic extremism and far right extremism pose a threat for the foreseeable future.[1] In addition, anti-abortion terrorism continues, and has become more deadly in the last few years.

The threat from Islamic terrorism

Islamic terrorism poses a threat to US interests at home and abroad. Here the focus is on the domestic threat. Islamic extremists hate the United States for what they see as its occupation of Saudi Arabia and its holy places, its blockade of Iraq, and its support for Israel. Osama bin Laden and his followers see themselves as fighting a *jihad* (holy war) against the United States. In 1998, the World Islamic Front for Jihad against Jews and Crusaders (Osama bin Laden's organization) declared: "To kill Americans and their allies – civilians and military – is an individual duty for every Muslim." Some writers think that religiously motivated terrorists are more willing than secular terrorists to carry out mass attacks against civilian targets (Stern 2000), since the victims are defined as unbelievers and infidels. A comparison with nationalist terrorists like the IRA or the Puerto Rican *independistas* suggests another explanation. The basic nationalist campaign strategy is to raise the cost in lives and money to the enemy, until the enemy leaves their land. The most obvious tactics are to kill the foreign soldiers who are occupying their land, and also to kill enemy civilians in their own homeland.[2] Osama bin Laden's followers have carried out both kinds of actions. They were responsible for attacks on American targets within the Muslim world: the 1993 ambush of marines in Somalia, the 1996 bombing of a US military complex in Dhahran, Saudi Arabia, the 1998 bombing of US embassies in Kenya and Tanzania, and the bombing of the USS *Cole* in Aden in 2000. They have also shown no qualms about attacking civilian targets in the United States. The 1993 bombing of the World Trade Center was intended to kill thousands of ordinary Americans. Subsequent efforts were foiled, but displayed the same ambition – to kill as many people as possible.[3] The old saying that "terrorists don't want lots of people dead, they want a lot of people watching" does not hold for groups that want to maximize the suffering of their enemy. The reason why it is the duty of every Muslim to kill American soldiers and civilians is explained by Osama bin Laden later in the declaration. Americans are to be killed "until the Aqsa Mosque [in Jerusalem] and the Haram Mosque [in Mecca] are freed from their grip and their armies, shattered and broken-winged, depart from all the lands of Islam."

The only limits then are their capabilities. There are probably tens of thousands of Muslims throughout the world who are willing to follow bin Laden's call. The more important question is: how many are there in the United States itself? It is reasonable to assume that the number is at least in the hundreds and perhaps in the thousands. This is due to incredibly inefficient immigration controls. The INS is overwhelmed by the sheer number of people entering the country, legally and illegally. Given the vigorous investigations by the FBI, and the current general watchfulness of the public, it is unlikely that any major action involving more than one or two men could be carried out. However, there is no reason to doubt that the remnants of the al Qaeda cells still in America (and others inspired by bin Laden's message) have the ability to carry out a variety of attacks. Assassinating elite individuals, or setting off bombs in public places, seem strong possibilities. Islamic extremists have attempted both in the past,[4] and either would have a major effect on public opinion.

The series of anthrax-contaminated letters are most likely being sent by a bin Ladenite cell or sympathizer. The timing suggests this, since the first letters were posted just after the September 11 attack. The alternative assumption – that it is the responsibility of right-wing extremists – requires that a *different* terrorist group coincidentally chose that time to send the letters, or had the anthrax letters ready to send off and decided in the aftermath of the September 11 attack that it was a good time to strike. Furthermore the letters appear to have been written by someone who is not a native English-speaker, and the message "Death to America. Death to Israel. Allah is great" in the anthrax-contaminated letters obviously suggests a Muslim. The disruption resulting from the letters was so great that, if the perpetrator has any more supplies of anthrax, we can anticipate more bioterrorism. On the other hand, it is doubtful that they have the capabilities at present to set off a nuclear weapon or start a smallpox epidemic. If they had such capabilities, I think they would have used them already.

The threat from the far right and anti-abortion terrorism

Unlike Islamic terrorists, both of these groups are made up of native-born Americans, so in evaluating the nature and extent of the threat from these groups it is important first to consider the domestic political situation, and the issues that arouse them.

The primary issue for the extreme right is the transformation of the United States from an overwhelmingly white English-speaking society into a multicultural society in which whites constitute a rapidly shrinking proportion of the population. Their hostility to this change is shared by many white Americans, as public opinion polls clearly show. A second factor, the so-called "culture wars," is also likely to generate increased support for the extreme right. On issues such as school prayer and homosexuality there is a marked disjunct between the general public and the political, business, and media elites. Although the anti-abortion movement is not part of the extreme right, there are some notable parallels between the political situation of the two.

On these issues, the political system has not responded to the concerns of the general public. Instead the government has usually ignored the majority position, passing laws and adopting policies that offend and anger many Americans. It is instructive to compare public opinion on immigration, English as the official language, prayer in school, homosexuality, and abortion with what the government has actually done on these issues.

Although the 1965 Immigration Act represented a radical change in the existing system, its congressional sponsors argued that the level of immigration would remain substantially unchanged, as would the ethnic composition of the immigrants. Both of these claims proved false. Although immigration law contains provision for immigrants to be deported if they become a public charge, the law is not enforced. Since the Border Patrol is grossly underfunded, illegal immigration is virtually uncontrolled. In 1986, over 3 million illegal immigrants were amnestied (Brimelow 1995: 76–8, 149, 236). After the 2000 census, the illegal immigrant total was estimated at over 7 million. The American public has opposed amnesty by large majorities, and for most of the period a plurality wanted the level of immigration reduced.[5] On the other hand, business welcomed the immigrants as a source of cheap labor, and as Brimelow (1995: 112) argues, "every major magazine and newspaper, and the leadership of both political parties remained adamantly in favor of immigration."

In the 1980s a movement to make English the official language of the United States emerged. The issue polarized many communities, and is generally condemned by liberals as nativist and "Hispanophobic."[6] In national surveys, support for English as the official language ranges between 60 percent and 80 percent. Referendums have usually won by equally large majorities. Proposition 63, to amend the state constitution to make English the official language of California, received 73 percent of the vote, and in Miami an antibilingual ordinance passed with 59 percent of the vote – in a city which was 40 percent Hispanic. As one critic of the Official English movement acknowledges, this "suggests a sizable nativist constituency" (Crawford 1992: xi).

Business groups, including the media, have been more than willing to cater to the growing Hispanic population. Business phones usually offer a Spanish language menu, and bilingual signs are everywhere. The media have been hostile to what they view as intolerance. "English-Only campaigns received unrelenting and largely unfavorable coverage in newspapers like the *Los Angeles Times*, the *Miami Herald* and the *Arizona Republic*" (Crawford 1992: 18).

The political system has been far from responsive to public concerns on the language issue: "Most politicians scrambled to avoid the issue . . . and Official English bills tended to expire in committee." The results of the referendums were ignored by state officials. In California, Attorney General Van de Kamp "who previously had fretted about the amendment's far-reaching impact now concluded that [Proposition 63] was purely advisory, without binding effect on voting, schooling, or any other public function" (Crawford 1992: 20). In several instances, policy on these nativist issues has been determined by the least democratic branch of government, the judiciary. In California in 1994, Proposition 187, an initiative designed to stop illegal immigrants using taxpayer-funded services, passed in a landslide, but was immediately struck down by a liberal judge. In California federal courts blocked attempts by local governments to impose the use of English on Spanish-speaking employees, and to prevent the display of Asian alphabet signs (Crawford 1992: 199, 203).

The first battle in the culture wars was over school prayers and Bible reading. The first amendment, "Congress shall make no law respecting an establishment of religion, or prohibiting the free exercise thereof," was historically interpreted in a minimalist fashion. Even after the revolution, several states had established churches, and most provided public funds to religious bodies and for religious education.[7] Not until 1962 did the Supreme Court prohibit prayers and Bible reading in public schools. The decision "startled and shocked millions of Americans who had grown accustomed to the association of God and country" (Laubach 1969: 150). Public opinion was heavily against the Supreme Court's decision. In a 1963 Gallup poll, 70 percent were opposed. A year later, the Survey Research Center reported that 74 percent approved of school prayer, 63 percent had only negative things to say about the Supreme Court, and that there were more negative mentions of the prayer issue than any other political issue (Laubach 1969: 138). Attempts were made to adopt a constitutional amendment, first by Representative Becker in 1963, and then by Senator Dirksen in 1966, but both failed.[8] The Supreme Court's position on school prayer, and church–state issues more generally, has fluctuated since the 1960s.

124 The future of American terrorism

In recent years the Court has softened its position on "the moment of silence" and has relaxed its position on equal access in the public schools to religious clubs and student groups.

The current cutting edge of the culture wars concerns homosexuality. Since the 1970s, over 200 cities and counties have adopted antidiscrimination measures protecting gays and lesbians. An increasing number of corporations, organizations, and municipalities have granted a range of benefits to the domestic partners of gays and lesbians. In 1991, Lotus Development Corporation became the first major business to do this, and by the end of the 1990s nearly 200 companies had done so, as well as some thirty municipalities, including New York City, Los Angeles, San Francisco, and Atlanta. This was clearly not in response to popular feeling. In a Gallup poll 53 percent thought homosexuality was "morally wrong" and nearly two-thirds disapproved of same-sex marriage. A 1992 *Newsweek* poll found that 65 percent opposed allowing gay couples to adopt, while in 1993 a *US News and World Report* poll found 70 percent opposed. Usually, whenever the issue has been put to the popular vote, the anti-gay side has won.

However, electoral victories by gay rights opponents[9] have often been blocked by the courts. In Colorado in 1992, an amendment to the state constitution which forbade governments at all levels to treat homosexuals or bisexuals as a class entitled to "minority status, quota preferences, protected status or claim of discrimination" passed by a vote of 814,000 to 710,000. The Supreme Court struck down the amendment by a six to three vote in 1996. Federal judges have aggressively struck down any laws that imply any negative judgement on homosexuality. In 1981 a Florida judge declared unconstitutional a state law that prevented homosexuals from adopting children, and in November 1995 the highest court in New York removed any bars to adoption by same-sex couples. In 1993, the Hawaii Supreme Court ruled that barring same-sex marriages amounted to sex discrimination. The media and the entertainment industry have been extremely sympathetic to the gay cause.

On these issues, there is a consistent pattern of majority preferences being ignored or thwarted. Given the failure of conventional political efforts, it is easy to see why – to some Americans – the government becomes the enemy, the militant option becomes more tempting, and more of these "extremists" resort to violence.

In some respects the abortion issue also fits this pattern. The Roe v. Wade decision of 1977 legalized abortion in the United States. A woman's right to have an abortion was derived from a right to privacy which seven of the justices discovered in the constitution. Public opinion has remained divided, with no obvious trend. According to the Gallup polls from 1975 to the present, on average about a quarter of those surveyed thought abortion should be legal under any circumstances, a sixth thought it should be illegal in all circumstances, and just over half thought it should be legal only under certain circumstances. Unlike the other issues, the political system has responded to the anti-abortion movement. Ever since Roe *v*. Wade was handed down, attempts began to overrule the Supreme Court by passing a human life amendment, although these attempts were blocked by liberal control of the House and Senate Judiciary Committees until Republicans won control of the Senate in 1980. More significant were congressional efforts, led by Representative Henry Hyde, to cut federal funding of abortions. In 1976 the federal government financed over 250,000 abortions at a cost of $50 million, but by 1978 only 2,328 abortions were federally funded at a cost of $777,158 (Steiner 1983: 33–5, 40). At the state level, Pro-life pressure achieved some success in passing bills that required the consent of husbands or parents before an abortion could be performed, although their implementation was often blocked by the courts (Steiner 1983: 23–4).

To ardent pro-lifers, however, the most important fact is that, in their eyes, more than a million unborn children are murdered every year. The right to demonstrate outside abortion clinics has been severely restricted under the Freedom of Access to Clinic Entrances Act of 1994. Under it the federal government could prosecute any anti-abortion civil disobedience that impeded clinic access. New York State's 1999 law was even more restrictive, and in the first case brought under the law a federal judge fined protestors $80,000 for "threatening behavior." Demonstrators have been arrested in thousands, and heavy fines and sentences imposed by judges. Media coverage of the anti-abortion movement is generally negative, reflecting the ideology of the media elite.[10] Police treatment of the civil rights movement in the 1960s was covered in vivid detail by television and newspapers and served to increase popular sympathy for the cause. The equally harsh treatment of anti-abortion protests is generally ignored.[11]

It can be assumed that nativist and moral issues will continue to generate large numbers of recruits for rightist and anti-abortion violence. There is likely to be a growing fusion between the two. Many on the extreme right are opposed to abortion. Eric Rudolph, the suspected bomber of the Olympic Park, also bombed an abortion clinic (and a gay bar). When Operation Rescue was being hounded by the courts to pay a $100,000 fine, and its financial assets were being threatened with seizure, Larry Pratt, one of the early leaders of the anti-government movement, came to its aid. Pratt allowed Operation Rescue to funnel its money through one of his organizations, the Committee to Protect the Family (Risen and Thomas 1998: 308–9). This was the beginning of several links that have developed between the militia movement and anti-abortion militants. The far right has attempted to recruit anti-abortionists to its cause, with claims that abortion is a Jewish conspiracy. Certainly in so far as the government defends abortionists and punishes them, the anti-government rhetoric of the far right must sound very appealing to anti-abortion activists.

The events of September 11 are likely to increase support for the extreme right for two reasons. First, since the attack was linked with US support for Israel, their antisemitic propaganda is likely to find a more receptive audience.[12] Second, the fact that the terrorists were Arab Muslims has created widespread hostility and suspicion towards aliens. Spontaneous attacks against "people who didn't look American" took place throughout the country, and indicated unease with racial diversity and multiculturalism. A Gallup poll taken the month after the September 11 attack showed that 58 percent wanted the level of immigration decreased, a jump of 17 percent from the previous survey. William Pierce, the leader of the National Alliance, declared that his message was at last being heard, and that the number of people who downloaded his weekly broadcast from the National Alliance web site had doubled since September 11 (*American Dissident Voices* October 20, 2001). Gordon Baum of the Council of Conservative Citizens said that there had been renewed interest in the group's anti-immigrant message (Pierre 2001).

The potential of the far right is weakened by its organizational disarray, since the movement is split by feuds based on both personality and ideological differences. Also heavy surveillance and infiltration by law enforcement make any coordinated action by a large group very difficult, if not impossible. Presumably we will see a continuation of isolated actions by lone wolves against various minorities. These so-called hate crimes are usually directed against randomly selected victims, and, despite their desperate and disorganized nature, such attacks have taken a lethal toll. In April 2000, Richard Bauhammers killed five people – his Jewish neighbor, three Asians, and one black – in a shooting rampage outside Pittsburgh PA.[13]

The Oklahoma City bombing by Timothy McVeigh may be an indication that such individuals are likely to strike at bigger targets than in the past, and to ignore the prospect of "collateral damage."[14] The extreme right has shown signs of interest in bioterrorism. A neo-Nazi internet newsletter published "Biology for Aryans" with details of botulism, anthrax, and typhoid. There have been a handful of well-publicized cases in which individuals linked with right-wing groups produced or obtained various deadly substances. In the 1980s the Covenant, the Sword, and the Arm of the Lord (CSA) stockpiled thirty gallons of cyanide, with which it supposedly intended to poison municipal water supplies. In March 1995 two members of the Minnesota Patriots' Council were arrested for possession of ricin. Also in 1995, Larry Wayne Harris, a microbiologist and former member of Aryan Nations, illegally bought three vials of bubonic plague from a commercial laboratory (Slevin 2001a; Stern 2000).[15]

But what would motivate far right extremists to use weapons of mass destruction? Stern (2000: 71–2) suggests that millenarian fantasies of a cleansing apocalypse may lead them to engage in terrorism to jump-start the process. She quotes a member of the CSA on why the group had planned to poison municipal reservoirs:

> We thought there were signs of Armageddon, and we believed that once those signs were there it was time for us to act. . . . The original timetable was up to God, but God could use us in creating Armageddon. That if we stepped out things might be hurried along. You got tired of waiting for what you think God is planning.

There are also more mundane rationales for right-wing extremists to use weapons of mass destruction. One terrorist strategy is that of "armed propaganda," in which acts of terrorism are intended to send a message and inspire others to carry out similar acts. The Oklahoma City bombing appears to fall into this category, although there is considerable uncertainty about Timothy McVeigh's precise motives and ideology.[16] McVeigh had contacts with militia groups, the Klan, and the National Alliance, and is alleged to have contacted the remnants of the CSA. His anger over Waco and the Ruby Ridge siege seems to have been the main reason why he decided to bomb the Murrah Federal Building, since it housed the offices of the FBI and BATF, who were involved in both incidents. The *Turner Diaries* by William Pierce obviously served as an inspiration for the attack, since it describes how an FBI building is blown up with a fuel oil and fertilizer truck bomb. Police even found photocopied pages of the book in McVeigh's car, with the following sentences highlighted: "The real value of our attacks lies in the psychological impact not in the immediate casualties. More important though is what we taught the politicians and the bureaucrats. They learned this afternoon that not one of them is beyond our reach." However, since the bombing led to public revulsion, it is unlikely that it will inspire copycat attacks. Most of those on the far right criticized the attack, not on moral grounds, but because it was counterproductive both in terms of public opinion and because it provided the government with a justification for a witch hunt against them. Indeed, several militia leaders alleged that the government itself had carried out the bombing in order to discredit the anti-government movement and create a crisis atmosphere in which new anti-terrorist legislation could be passed.

Another strategy in which weapons of mass destruction might be used by right-wing extremists is to provoke a race war, and the concept has even been given an acronym, RAHOWA (Racial Holy War). In 1993, members of the Fourth Reich skinheads were arrested and accused of conspiring to assassinate black leaders and bomb black churches in the hope that blacks would respond by attacking whites, leading to mass racial conflict ("LA race war plot" 1993). Given the high degree of residential racial segregation in the United States, the standard objection to using chemical, biological, or nuclear weapons – that you would harm your own people – would not have much weight. Fortunately, there is no evidence to suggest that right-wing groups or individuals have the capabilities to carry out such attacks.

A separatist strategy of creating a white homeland has been proposed by several right-wing leaders. Harold Covington calls for "racially conscious" whites to relocate to the Pacific Northwest. Once in the area they would engage in a program of political action and propaganda. "Eventually there must be direct action to remove as much of the territory of the Northwest as possible from the jurisdiction and control of the United States and subsequently create an independent Aryan Republic" (www.northwestagency.com). A southern separatist movement is growing, with the League of the South and the Southern Party openly working towards secession. Southern heritage groups such as the Sons of Confederate Veterans have been penetrated by right-wing and racist elements (Breed 2001). Although one may dismiss these separatist schemes as unrealistic, they have the potential to inspire violence wherever local concentrations of sympathizers exist.

Counterterrorism policies: some modest proposals

Counterterrorist policies can be classified along two dimensions. The first is the cost of a policy in terms of not only money but also public inconvenience. The second is the risk reduction effected by the policy (i.e. how much increased security does it produce?). The ideal policy is one which substantially reduces risk at a low economic and social cost. On the other hand, policies which are costly but do little to improve security are to be avoided.

Target-hardening proposals lend themselves to a fairly simple cost/benefit analysis of these two factors. How much is risk reduced and what is the cost of the increased security? Sharply diminishing returns to increased security should be expected after the most important targets have been protected, since terrorists can always drop down to the next level of less well protected targets. For example, although the British were able to develop a sophisticated defense system for the City of London itself, the IRA merely shifted its efforts to satellite financial institutions located *outside* the City. By all means tighten security at nuclear power plants, airports,[17] etc., but the assumption that every bus terminal, train station, and bridge can be guarded is an illusion.

Machines now exist that can videotape faces and match them with known terrorists. Advanced x-ray scanners can pick up items as small as a razor blade by the difference in density of various materials. Identities can be checked against hand prints or the retina of an eye. Advanced technological devices cannot, however, substitute for well prepared and trained personnel. The federal government spent well over $2 billion to upgrade security at federal buildings after the Oklahoma City bombing. However, undercover agents from the General Accounting Office were able to bypass security checkpoints at federal buildings in Washington DC by posing as police officers. They attempted to penetrate nineteen buildings and were successful every time, even walking past guards at such high-security sites as the Pentagon, the CIA, and the Department of Justice. In other reviews, the GAO found that private security guards had not had proper security checks or firearms training, while one audit found "dozens of x-ray machines, closed-circuit televisions and magnetometers were delivered but still unpacked two years after purchase" (Tucker and Dvorak 2001: A12).

Profiling is generally condemned as *a very bad thing*. In fact it is the basis of all good law enforcement. Instead of inconveniencing the general public and creating widespread disaffection, law enforcement efforts are focused where they are most likely to prevent terrorism and catch terrorists. Since the main threat at present comes from Muslim terrorists, then obviously the Muslim community should be singled out for special attention. However, while justifiable in the short term as an emergency response, intrusive general surveillance of Muslims should be replaced as soon as possible by more discriminating policies. The key to successful counterterrorism is good intelligence, and the most effective way of getting intelligence is through the use of informers. The FBI apparently was unable to develop intelligence sources in the Muslim and Arab-American communities prior to, or even after, the 1993 World Trade Center bombing. The FBI has almost no Arab-American agents, and after the September 11 attacks it had to put out a request for people able to translate confiscated Arabic language documents and wiretaps. The agency is making strenuous efforts to develop contacts with the Muslim community (Slevin 2001b). Many will regard the willingness of Muslim leaders to encourage their followers to cooperate with law enforcement as a measure of their loyalty to the country.

One obvious way of reducing the threat from foreign terrorists is to tighten immigration controls. All the hijackers in the September 11 attacks obtained tourist or business visas, and several of them over-stayed their time limits. The screening process is clearly ineffective, and there is no way of locating and deporting those who remain in the country illegally. The pilot of the plane that rammed into the Pentagon was admitted on a student visa to take a four-week English course at a California college, but never showed up for classes. Although visa applicants are supposedly checked against a State Department database, the Consular Lookout and Support System, the system is flawed and is not even linked to the FBI's databases. Sheik Omar Abdel Rahman, found guilty of conspiracy in the 1993 World Trade Center bombing, was granted a visa despite being on the lookout list. Two of the Pentagon hijackers were identified as potential terrorists, but were admitted to the country and then disappeared (Schemo and Pear 2001; Gugliotta 2001). Any extra security spending to hire more INS personnel would be valuable in reducing the risk that foreign terrorists could slip into the country.

Although some analysts have criticized what they regard as an over-emphasis on weapons of mass destruction, it is clear that nuclear terror-ism and biological terrorism pose a real threat. Furthermore, as the anthrax letters have shown, even experts are unaware of all potential hazards, so it would be wise to err on the side of caution. In June 2001, federal officials tried to assess how the health system would cope with a smallpox outbreak, by simulating the spread of the disease from an initial twenty-four infected individuals. The simulation, code-named "Dark Winter," indicated that within two weeks 15,000 people would have become infected, and the computer model predicted ultimate chaos as the epidemic overwhelmed efforts to contain it. Should terrorists obtain a nuclear bomb or enough radioactive materials to make a "dirty bomb" by wrapping them around conventional explosives, the loss of life and disruption would be equally severe. However, there are some obvious and relatively low-cost ways of reducing the risk of either of these situations occurring. Since the United States does not have enough doses of smallpox vaccine to cope with even a small outbreak, it should produce more vaccines as rapidly as possible. Because Russia is generally regarded as the most likely source of nuclear materials for terrorists, the Nunn–Lugar Cooperative Threat Reduction Program of 1991 has attempted to upgrade security at Russian nuclear and biological research facilities, to destroy dangerous materials, and make sure that impoverished Russian scientists are not tempted to sell their expertise abroad. This eminently sensible program should be maintained and expanded.

Until the Antiterrorism Act of 1996 and the recently enacted Patriot Act, the United States did not have any special legislation dealing with terrorism. Now the United States like other Western democracies has created a special class of terrorist crimes, given the police special powers, and even created special courts to try terrorists. For democracies threatened by terrorism, security concerns and civil liberties are often in conflict. Again a cost/benefit perspective is appropriate. Previous research suggests that security legislation should be narrowly focused and as unintrusive as possible. One of the most useful tools of law enforcement is a reliable method of identifying who people are. A national identity card would be invaluable for this purpose, and the inconvenience to most of the general public would be minimal. For most Americans their social security number or driver's license serves as their ID and they give and show these frequently to all sorts of people without feeling that their civil liberties are being violated. Some recent changes seem sensible – for example, allowing the FBI and intelligence agencies to exchange information, or allowing federal agents to wiretap any phone that a suspect uses rather than having to obtain a separate court order for each phone. However, the executive order of November 13, 2001, is drafted in such a sweeping fashion that large numbers of people are potentially subject to detention without trial, a most arbitrary and draconian deprivation of their freedom. According to Philip Heymann, a former deputy US Attorney General, the order covers 18 million foreign-born non-US citizens if "the president suspects that one of them may have been a terrorist in the past, or is a terrorist, or has aided a terrorist, or has harbored a terrorist, even decades ago" (Lardner 2001: A10). This would appear to be an example of the kind of policy to be avoided.

Two general points should be made about terrorism in America. First, counterterrorism policy should not *overemphasize* weapons of mass destruction and spectacular events. Most terrorism is small-scale, carried out by a handful of people or even a single individual. Most terrorist attacks result in minor damage, and usually cause no fatalities. Terrorist casualties overall are minor compared with those caused by other natural and social disasters. Second, although the September 11 attack was followed by a resolve to crush terrorism wherever it existed, history suggests that complete victory is unlikely. Terrorism is a product of frustration, of causes that cannot be resolved through normal politics. Even though Osama bin Laden and al Qaeda may be destroyed, other causes will emerge to inspire other terrorists. The history of terrorism shows that, even as society learns new ways to defend itself, the terrorists will invent new tactics.

Notes

1 There is also potential for increased and more deadly terrorism by animal rights activists and radical environmentalists. See Barcott (2002).
2 The campaigns of the IRA, ETA, the Puerto Rican FALN and other nationalist groups have targeted both enemy soldiers and enemy civilians.
3 The 1993 bombing was intended to topple the World Trade Center, and in the same year the FBI arrested a group who were planning to blow up other New York buildings and set off bombs in the Lincoln and Holland tunnels. In December 1999, an Algerian was arrested with explosive materials in his car when he tried to cross the border from Canada. He told police that he planned to bomb Los Angeles International Airport.
4 The assassination of Robert Kennedy and that of Rabbi Meir Kahane are two examples.
5 Since the 1965 Immigration Act, the number seeking a decrease has ranged from 33 percent to 65 percent with the average of eleven surveys being 49 percent. Those wanting an increase averaged only 9 percent, while on average 32 percent were in favor of the current level (see www.gallup.com).
6 Crawford (1992: 5,101,163) gives several examples of such hostility. In a survey of contributors to US English, 42 percent agreed with the statement "I want America to stand tall and not cave in to Hispanics who shouldn't be here."
7 Laubach (1969), who supports the Supreme Court's decision, entitles his first chapter "Rediscovery of the First Amendment," implying that the amendment had been misunderstood for 170 years.
8 Senator Dirksen "prophesied that Christmas programs, carols, and nativity scenes might eventually be excluded from public schools" but Senator Bayh thought this was a "ludicrous interpretation" (Laubach 1969: 141,

143). The most recent Gallup survey found that 66 percent favored "daily prayer in the classroom."

9 Of nineteen gay rights-issues on local ballots since 1998, gay-rights foes won fourteen.

10 Lichter *et al.* (1986) found that 90 percent of his sample of the media elite were pro-choice.

11 For example, in spring 1989 the Los Angeles Police Department used pain compliance techniques to break up anti-abortion demonstrations. "Police officers used *nunchaku* (martial arts sticks) to grab and drag their prisoners and at least one protester's arm was broken . . . charges of police brutality during the Holy Week campaign were virtually ignored by the mainstream media" (Risen and Thomas 1998: 288).

12 According to a poll released by the ADL on their web site www.adl.org there has been no increase in antisemitism in the wake of the September 11 attacks. Only 22 percent of those surveyed believe that the attack would not have occurred if the United States were not such a close ally of Israel, and only 25 percent thought that "Jews are more loyal to Israel than America."

13 The exact numbers are uncertain, since some actions were carried out by people who had a history of mental illness, and it is therefore difficult to determine whether ideology was their primary motivation. Although most of his victims were interracial couples, Joseph Paul Franklin also shot and wounded Vernon Jordan and Larry Flynt. It should be noted that William Pierce, the leader of the National Alliance, has criticized such leaderless resistance as ineffective, and even counterproductive, since it justifies censorship and repression of the extreme right.

14 McVeigh dismissed the deaths of the children killed in the bombing with this phrase.

15 Harris was convicted of mail fraud, since he had misrepresented himself in his purchase order.

16 On McVeigh and the Oklahoma City bombing see Stickney (1996), Jones (1998), Hoffman (1998), and Michel and Herbeck (2001).

17 Although desirable measures such as increased airport security have a "bolting the stable door after the horse has gone" quality, since lax airport security has been criticized for years.

Appendix
Data sources and coding procedures

The data set is based on several kinds of published sources. Initially, I used general chronologies starting with Trick (1976) for the 1965–76 period, those in the *Annual of Power and Conflict* (1976–81), and the FBI's annual reports, which begin in 1980.[1] In addition, useful sources on particular ideological waves of terrorism include the following.

For Klan terrorism, the House Committee on Un-American Activities report, *The Present Day Ku Klux Klan Movement* (1967), Bullard (1989, 1998), Newton and Newton (1991), and Nelson (1993). The most comprehensive chronology of leftist and black violence covering the 1965–70 period is in *Scanlans* (1971). Sources for particular groups include Heath (1976), Epstein (1971), and Pearson (1994) on the Black Panthers, Howard (1979) on the Zebra killings, Castellucci (1986) on the M19CO group, and McLellan (1977) on the Symbionese Liberation Army. For Puerto Rican terrorism, Sater (1981) provides a good chronology, and Fernandez (1987, 1994) covers the activities of the Macheteros. There are two chronologies of Jewish violence and terrorism, Sater (1996) and Russ (1981), as well as a good study of the Jewish Defense League by Friedman (1990). Statistics on Cuban terrorism are given in Herman (1980), Garcia (1996), and Uriarte-Gaston (1984). Anti-abortion violence is documented in detail by the National Abortion Federation. The violent activities of the New Right are closely monitored by watchdog groups, the most important of which are the SPLC and the ADL. Their reports are the main source of information on racist and antisemitic violence. See, for example, *Ku Klux Klan: A history of racism and violence* by the SPLC, and *Shaved for Battle: Skinheads target America's youth*, and *Hate Groups in America* by the ADL. Additional sources include Melnichak (1991), Flynn *et al.* (1989), Hamm (1993), and Coates (1987).

The *Reader's Guide to Periodicals*, *Keesing's*, *Facts on File*, and the *New York Times index* were searched for any reported incidents of terrorism, arrests, and trials of terrorists. Finally, phone calls were made to local newspapers, and a web search was made for missing and additional material. I would like to thank the *Cleveland Plain Dealer*, the *San Juan Star*, the *Miami Herald*, and the *Dayton Daily News* for their help.[2] Thanks also to the Fraternal Order of Police for their assistance in identifying law enforcement personnel killed by terrorists and extremists.

I generally accepted all recorded violent incidents in which there was any evidence of political or social motivation as "terrorist" except in the following cases:

1   The person carrying out the attack appears to have been motivated by selfish criminal motives.
2   Spontaneous violence by unorganized crowds, or unpremeditated fights between individuals, were not considered terrorism.
3   Trivial attacks were ignored. All bombings and shooting incidents were considered non-trivial, as were kidnapings and robberies. Arson and vandalism if resulting in less than $1,000 damage were considered trivial. Assaults were included if the victim was hospitalized, described as severely injured, or where serious injuries were implied (e.g. "beaten by an iron bar").[3]

I took as evidence of political or social motivation any one of the following:

1   The fact that a group claimed the attack, or was identified by law enforcement agencies as responsible for the attack.
2   The individuals carrying out the attack were members of an extremist group.
3   The individuals carrying out the attack gave an ideological reason for the attack, or the targets were apparently selected for ideological reasons.

The ultimate sources for almost all data on terrorism are government records and media reports. Two possible biases are that incidents may not be recorded or not recognized as terrorist in nature. It is likely that certain types of terrorism are more likely to be reported and identified as terrorist. Law enforcement officials and journalists are often unaware that a particular robbery was perpetrated by a terrorist group rather than by ordinary criminals. According to Mizell (1998) terrorists robbed at least 368 banks and armored cars during 1977–97, while my chronology for a longer time period contains about half that number.

Although white racist actions are closely monitored, black racist crimes are often not identified as such, sometimes because the attacks are confused with normal street crime.[4] Often the media appear reluctant to publicize or identify hate crimes by blacks.[5]

The data are organized into three files:

1 *Terrorist incidents.* Over 3,000 incidents with information on date, place (state and locality), type of action, target, perpetrator, and outcome (killed and wounded, property damage, etc.). Those responsible are identified by group, if known, or by general ideological category if not. Groups are also classified by ideology; thus all black groups are listed under an acronym that begins with a B (e.g. BLA: Black Liberation Army), all Jewish groups with a J (e.g. JDL: Jewish Defense League), etc.

2 *Terrorist-related fatalities.* In addition to above information on date, place, perpetrator, and type of incident this data set contains further information on victims, including name, age, gender, race, and why killed.

3 *Terrorist trials and sentences.* Contains information on named terrorists tried, the outcome of the trial, and the sentence. Terrorists are classified by organizational affiliations/ideology. Biographical data are available for a small percentage of individuals.

For further information on these data sets, please contact: Professor Christopher Hewitt, Department of Sociology, University of Maryland, Baltimore County, 1000 Hilltop Circle, Baltimore MD 21250. E-mail: hewitt@umbc.edu.

Notes

1 The FBI statistics obviously begin much earlier because the agency – as early as the 1970s – several times made announcements about the number of terrorist incidents from year to year, but this information has not been published.

2 For example, Neil Bradley Long, a lone racist gunman, killed and wounded several blacks in Dayton OH over a period of months, but the national media accounts were skimpy and contradictory, so I contacted the *Dayton Daily News*, which provided me with full details.

3 This criterion significantly reduces the number of anti-abortion attacks against abortion clinics, although it generally agrees with what the National Abortion Federation classifies as incidents of "extreme violence."

4 Pearsall (1974: 1) in his study of the SLA notes that "the characteristic crime of violence in the [San Francisco] area typically involves a black as the criminal and a white as the victim."

5 The *Washington Post*, for example, published a lengthy article on the black Yahweh cult, members of which murdered several whites, without mentioning the race of their victims. After Kevin Shifflett, an eight-year-old white boy, was murdered by Gregory Murphy, a black man, anti-white writings were found in the killer's room. However, subsequent articles on the horrific crime virtually ignored its racial aspects. For a defense of the paper's coverage of the case see Shipp (2000). The *Washington Post*'s coverage of the Shifflett murder can be compared with its treatment of the shooting rampage by Buford Furrow. While both Murphy and Furrow appear to have been mentally ill, Furrow's links with white racist groups were emphasized repeatedly.

Bibliography

Achenbach, J. (2001) "The enemies may change but the hate lives on" *Washington Post* September 13: C4.

Adams, N. (1993) "The terrorists among us" *Reader's Digest* December: 74–80.

Aho, J. (1990) *The Politics of Righteousness: Idaho Christian patriotism*, Seattle WA: University of Washington Press.

Anthony, E. (1990) *Spitting in the Wind: The true story behind the legacy of the Black Panther Party*, Santa Monica CA: Roundtable Publishers.

Barcott, B. (2002) "From tree hugger to terrorist" *New York Times Magazine* April 7: 56–9, 81.

Barkun, M. (1994) *Religion and the Racist Right*, Chapel Hill NC: University of North Carolina Press.

Bates, T. (1992) *RADS: The 1970 bombing of the Army Math Research Center*, New York: Harper Collins.

Becker, J. (1978) *Hitler's Children*, New York: Granada Publishing.

Berke, R. and Elder, J. (2001) "Poll finds strong support for US use of military force" *New York Times* September 16: 6.

Bernstein, R. (1994) "Hate literature documents weighed in bombing trial" *New York Times* January 27: B4.

Berry, J. (2001) "Loss of confidence threatens economy" *Washington Post* September 29: E5.

"Black mood: more militant, more hopeful" (1970) *Time* April 6.

Blanchard, D. and Prewitt, T. (1993) *Religious Violence and Abortion*, Gainesville FL: University of Florida.

"Blast" (1977) *New Yorker* October 24: 35–6.

Bock, A. (1995) *Ambush at Ruby Ridge*, Irvine CA: Dickens Press.

Bowman, S. (1994) *When the Eagle Screams*, Secaucus NJ: Carol Publishing.

Boyer, P. (1999) "Burned" *New Yorker* November 1: 62–8.

Breed, A. (2001) "Battle brews for soul of Confederate group" *Washington Post* December 14: A59.

Brimelow, P. (1995) *Alien Nation*, New York: Random House.

Broadway, B. (2001) "Number of US Muslims depends on who's counting" *Washington Post* November 24: A1.

Browning, R. (1990) *Racial Politics in American Cities*, New York: Longman.

Bullard, S. (1989) *Free at Last: A history of the civil rights movement*, Montgomery AL: Southern Poverty Law Center.

Bullard, S. (1998) *Ku Klux Klan: A history of racism and violence*, Montgomery AL: Southern Poverty Law Center.

Burghart, D. and Crawford, R. (1996) *Guns and Gavels*, Portland OR: Coalition for Human Dignity.

Canedy D. (2001) "Crop-dusters are grounded on fears of toxic attacks" *New York Times* September 25: B5.

Cannistraro, V. (2001) "Undetected at home" *Washington Post* September 13: A31.

Castellucci, F. (1986) *The Big Dance: The untold story of Kathy Boudin and the terrorist family that committed the Brinks robbery*, New York: Dodd Mead.

Chesnoff, R. (1993) "Between bombers and believers" *US News & World Report* September 20: 34–5.

Claiborne, W. (2000) "Supremacy group faces fateful trial" *Washington Post* August 28: A3.

Clarke, J. W. (1982) *American Assassins: The darker side of politics*, Princeton NJ: Princeton University Press.

Clegg, C. (1997) *An Original Man: The life and times of Elijah Muhammad*, New York: St Martin's Press.

Coates, J. (1987) *Armed and Dangerous: The rise of the survivalist right*, New York: Hill and Wang.

Cohen, S. M. (1984) *The 1984 Survey of American Jews*, New York: American Jewish Committee.

Conlin, J. (1982) *The Troubles: A jaundiced glance back at the movement of the '60s*, New York: Franklin Watts.

Craig, B. (1993) *Abortion and American Politics*, Chatham NJ: Chatham House.

Crawford, J. (1992) *Hold your Tongue: Bilingualism and the politics of "English Only,"* New York: Addison-Wesley.

Crenshaw, M. (1988) "Theories of terrorism: instrumental and organizational approaches" in D. Rapoport (ed.) *Inside Terrorist Organizations*, New York: Columbia University Press.

"Cuban exiles: Miami, haven for terror" (1977) *Nation* March 19: 326–31.

Daley, R. (1973) *Target Blue*, New York: Delacorte Press.

Dannen, F. (1996) "The G-man and the hit man" *New Yorker* December 16: 68–77.

Davies, J. C. (1971) *When Men Revolt and Why*, New York: Free Press.

Dees, M. (1996) *Gathering Storm*, New York: Harper Collins.

Dees, M. and Potok, M. (2001) "The future of American terrorism" *New York Times* July 10: 15.

Degenhardt, H. (1983) *Political Dissent*, Detroit MI: Gale Research.

"Deliberate strategy of disruption" (2001) *Washington Post* November 4.

DeYoung, K. and Dobbs, M. (2001) "Bin Laden: architect of new global terrorism" *Washington Post* September 16: A8.

Diamond, S. (1995) *Roads to Dominion: Right-wing movements and political power in the United States*, New York: Guildford Press.

Didion, J. (1987) *Miami*, New York: Simon & Schuster.

Dobratz, B. and Shanks-Meile, S. (1997) *"White Power, White Pride!": The white separatist movement in the United States*, New York: Twayne Publishers.

Downs, A. (1957) *Economic Theory of Democracy*, New York: Harper.

Duggan, P. (1999) "Tearing down a fence and more: racist killing forces Jasper, Texas, to look hatred in the eye" *Washington Post* January 26: A3.

Edsall, T. (2001a) "Anti-Muslim violence assailed" *Washington Post* September 15: A9.

Edsall, T. (2001b) "Attacks shift balance of power alliances among interest groups" *Washington Post* September 19: A6.

Emerson, S. (1995) "The other fundamentalists" *New Republic* June 12.

Epstein, E. (1971) "C. R. Garry's list of Panthers allegedly killed by police" *New Yorker* February 13: 45–6.

Essien-Udom, E. (1962) *Black Nationalism*, Chicago: University of Chicago Press.

Etzioni, A. (1999) "Words on the Web" *Washington Post* February 20: A17.

Fagen, R., Brady, R. and O'Leary, T. (1968) *Cubans in Exile*, Stanford, CA: Stanford University Press.

"FBI's toughest foe: the kids" (1970) *Newsweek* 76 October 26: 22–3.

"Fear in the streets of San Francisco" (1974) *Time* April 29: 18.

Fernandez, R. (1987) *Los Macheteros*, New York: Prentice-Hall.

Fernandez, R. (1994) *Prisoners of Colonialism*, Monroe ME: Common Courage Press.

Finnegan, W. (1998) "Defending the unabomber" *New Yorker* March 16.

Fisher, J. (1997) *Killer Among Us: Public reactions to serial murder*, Westport CT: Praeger.

Flynn, K. and Gerhardt, G. (1989) *The Silent Brotherhood: Inside America's racist underground*, New York: Free Press.

Friedly, M. (1992) *Malcolm X: The assassination*, New York: Caroll & Graf.

Friedman, R. I. (1990) *False Prophet: Rabbi Meir Kahane*, New York: Lawrence Hill Books.

Friedman, T. (2001a) "Muslim nations must oppose own extremists" *Baltimore Sun* September 18: 21A.

Friedman, T. (2001b) "The big terrible" *New York Times* September 18: A31.

Garcia, M. C. (1996) *Havana USA: Cuban exiles in south Florida*, Berkeley CA: University of California Press.

Gay, K. (1997) *Militias: Armed and dangerous*, Springfield NJ: Enslow Publishers.

George, J. and Wilcox, L. (1992) *Nazis, Communists, Klansmen, and Others on the Fringe*, Buffalo NY: Prometheus.

Gerbner, G. (1991) "Symbolic functions of violence and terror" in Y. Alexander and R. Pickard (eds) *In the Camera's Eye*, Washington DC: Brassey's.

Golden, T., Moss M. and Yardley, J. (2001) "Unpolished agents were able to hide out in plain sight" *New York Times* September 23.

Goldman, P. (1970) *Report from Black America*, New York: Simon & Schuster.

Goldman, P. (1979) *The Death and Life of Malcolm X*, Urbana IL: University of Illinois Press.

Goldstein, A. (2001) "Blood donations easing shortage" *Washington Post* September 18: A24.

Goodell, C. (1973) *Political Prisoners in America*, New York: Random House.

Granberg, D. (1981) "The abortion activists" *Family Planning Perspectives* 13 July/August: 157–63.

Gugliotta, G. (2001) "Terrorism watch list was no match for hijackers" *Washington Post* September 23: A22.

Guth, J. (1994) "Cut from the whole cloth: antiabortion mobilization among religious activists" in T. Jelen and M. Chandler (eds) *Abortion Politics in the US and Canada*, Westport CT: Praeger.

Hamm, M. (1993) *American Skinheads: The criminology and control of hate crime*, Westport CT: Praeger.

Handler, J. (1990) "Socioeconomic profile of an American terrorist, 1960s and 1970s" *Terrorism* 13: 195–214.

Hashmi, S. (2001) "The terrorists' zealotry is political, not religious" *Washington Post* September 30: B1.

Hate Groups in America: A record of bigotry and violence (1988) New York: Anti-defamation League of B'Nai B'rith.

Heath, G. L. (1976) *Off the Pigs!*, Metuchen NJ: Scarecrow Press.

Herman, R. (1980) "Highest priority given to capture of anti-Castro group" *New York Times* March 3: A1, 3.

Heymann, P. (1998) *Terrorism and America*, Boston MA: MIT Press.

"Hijack suspects mostly blended in" (2001) *Washington Post* September 16.

"Hijackers had a careful strategy of brains, muscle and practice" (2001) *New York Times* November 4: B6

Hoffman, B. (1986) "Terrorism in the United States during 1985" *TVI Journal*.

Hoffman, B. (1998) *Inside Terrorism*, New York: Columbia University Press.

"Holy war" (1973) *Newsweek* February 5.

Horowitz, T. (1999) "Run, Rudolph, run" *New Yorker* March 15.

Howard, C. (1979) *Zebra*, New York: Marek.

Huntingdon, S. (1996) *The Clash of Civilizations and the Remaking of World Order*, New York: Simon & Schuster.

"Is the US next?" (1978) *Newsweek* May 22: 38.

Janke, P. (1983) *Guerrilla and Terrorist Organisations: A world directory and bibliography*, New York: Macmillan.

Jeffers, H. P. (1972) *Wanted by the FBI*, New York: Hawthorne Books.

Jenkins, R. (1997) *Blind Vengeance: The Roy Moody mail bomb murders*, Athens GA: University of Georgia Press.

Johnson, L. (2001) "The declining terrorist threat" *New York Times* July 10: 15.

Joint Center for Political Studies (1977) *Profiles of Black Mayors in America*, Washington DC: JCPS.

Jones, S. (1998) *Others Unknown: The Oklahoma City bombing case and conspiracy*, New York: Public Affairs Press.

Jongman, A. J. and Schmid, A. P. (1984) *World Directory of Terrorist and Other Organizations Associated with Guerrilla Warfare, Political Violence and Protest*, New Brunswick NJ: Transaction Books.

Kaplan, J. (1995) "Absolute rescue: absolutism, defensive action and the resort to force" *Terrorism and Political Violence* 7: 128–56.

Kaplan, J. (1997) *Radical Religion in America: Millenarian movements from the far right to the Children of Noah*, Syracuse NY: Syracuse University Press.

Kaplan, D. and Tharp, M. (1998) "Terrorism threats at home" *US News & World Report* January 5: 22–7.

Kaufman, M. (1973) "Slaying of one of the last Black Liberation Army members still at large" *New York Times* November 16: 10.

Kelly, M. (1996) "Playing with fire" *New Yorker* July 15.

Klaidman, D. (1996) "The Feds' quiet war" *Newsweek* April 22.

Klehr, H. (1986) *Biographical Dictionary of the American Left*, Westport CT: Greenwood Press.

Kurtz, H. (1987) "FBI memo: Israelis hampering probe" *Washington Post* November 19: A19.

Kushner, H. (1998) *Terrorism in America*, Springfield IL: Charles C. Thomas.

"LA race war plot" (1993) *USA Today* July 16–18: A1.

Lancaster, J. (2001) "Senate Democrats, White House reach a deal on anti-terror Bill" *Washington Post* October 4.

Langer, E. (1990) "The American neo-Nazi movement today" *Nation* July 16.

Laqueur, W. (1977) *Terrorism*, Boston MA: Little Brown.

Lardner, G. (2001) "Legal scholars criticize wording of Bush order" *Washington Post* December 3: A10.

Larsen, J. (1985) "Son of Brinks," *New York* May 6.

Laubach, J. (1969) *School Prayers: Congress, the courts, and the public*, Washington DC: Public Affairs Press.

Leo, J. (2001) "A war of two worlds" *US News & World Report* September 24: 47.

Leonhardt, D. (2001) "A body blow to the economy" *New York Times* September 16.

Lewis, C. (2000) "The terror that failed: public opinion in the aftermath of the bombing in Oklahoma City" *Public Administration Review* 60: 201–10.

Lichter, S. R., Rothman, S. and Lichter, L. S. (1986) *The Media Elite*, Bethesda MD: Adler & Adler.

Lipset, S. M. (1963) *The First New Nation: The United States in historical and comparative perspective*, New York: Basic Books.

Lipset, S. M. (1989) *Continental Divide: The values and institutions of the United States and Canada*, Washington DC: Canadian American Committee.

Lukas, J. (1970) "On the Lam in America" *New York Times Magazine* December 13: 30.

Luker, K. (1984) *Abortion and the Politics of Motherhood*, Berkeley CA: University of California Press.

Magnusson, E. (1985) "Explosions over abortion" *Time* January 14: 16–17.

"Malice towards some" (1966) *Newsweek* 67 April 11: 39–40.

Marino, J. (1999) "Apology isn't enough for Puerto Rico spy victims" *Washington Post* December 28: A3.

Martin, W. (1996) *With God on Our Side: The rise of the religious right in America*, New York: Broadway Books.

Martire, G. (1982) *Anti-Semitism in the United States*, New York: Praeger.

Masotti, L. (1969) *Shootout in Cleveland*, Washington DC: US Government Printing Office.

Massengill, R. (1994) *Portrait of a Racist*, New York: St Martin's Press.

Maynard, M. (2001) "Airlines' bad year is suddenly looking much, much worse" *New York Times* September 16.

McLellan, V. (1977) *The Voices of Guns*, New York: Putnam.

McMillen, N. (1971) *The Citizens' Councils*, Urbana IL: University of Illinois Press.

Melnichak, J. (1991) "A chronicle of hate" *TVI Report* 6: 38–42.

Memmott, M. (2001) "Poll finds a united nation" *USA Today* September 17: 4A.

Michel, L. and Herbeck, D. (2001) *American Terrorist: Timothy McVeigh and the Oklahoma City bombing*, New York: Regan Books.

Milloy, C. (2001) "Terrorism feeds on the global suffering we too often ignore" *Washington Post* September 19: B1.

Mizell, L. (1998) *Target USA: The inside story of the new terrorist war*, New York: Wiley.

Monroe, C. (1982) "Addressing terrorism in the United States" *Annals of the American Academy of Political Science* September: 141 7.

"Montana outrage stalls skinheads" (1994) *New York Times* February 20: 38.

Morgenthau, T. (1994) "A terrorist plot without a story" *Newsweek* February 28: 28–9.

Mullins, W. (1988) *Terrorist Organizations in the United States*, Springfield IL: Thomas.

Mullins, W. (1993) "Hate crime and the far right," in K. Tunnell (ed.) *Political Crime in Contemporary America,* New York: Garland.

Nacos, B. (1994) *Terrorism and the Media*, New York: Columbia University Press.

National Advisory Committee on Criminal Justice Standards and Goals, Task Force on Disorders and Terrorism (NACCJSG) (1976) *Disorders and Terrorism*, Washington DC: US Government Printing Office.

Nelson, A. (1986) *Murder under Two Flags*, New York: Tickner & Fields.

Nelson, J. (1993) *Terror in the Night: The Klan's campaign against the Jews*, New York: Simon & Schuster.

Newfield, J. (1966) *A Prophetic Minority*, New York: New American Library.

Newton, M. and Newton, J. (1991) *Racial and Religious Violence in America*, New York: Garland.

Okie, S. (2001) "Use of anti-anxiety drugs jumps in US" *Washington Post* October 14: A8.

Ollove, M. (2001) "Everything changed yesterday" *Baltimore Sun* September 12: 1A.

"Open season on Panthers?" (1969) *Christian Century* 86: 1634.

"Out to get the Panthers" (1969) *Nation* 209 July 28: 78–82.

Paletz, D., Azanian, J. and Fozzard, P. (1982) "Terrorism on TV news" in William Adams (ed.) *Television Coverage of International Affairs*, Norwood NJ: Ablex.

Parry, A. (1976) *Terrorism from Robespierre to Arafat*, New York: Vanguard Press.

Paterson, T. (1994) *Contesting Castro*, New York: Oxford University Press.

Patterson, E. (1974) *Black City Politics*, New York: Dodd Mead.

Pearlstein, R. (1991) *The Mind of the Political Terrorist*, Wilmington DE: SR Books.

Pearlstein, S. (2001) "Risk factors taking a toll on economy" *Washington Post* October 5: E1, 5.

Pearsall, R. (1974) *The Symbionese Liberation Army*, Amsterdam: Rodopi.

Pearson, H. (1994) *The Shadow of the Panther*, Reading MA: Addison-Wesley.

"Persecution and assassination of the Black Panthers" (1969) *Ramparts Magazine* 7 January 25: 120–6.

Picard, R. and Adams, P. (1987) "Characterizations of acts and perpetrators of political violence in three elite US daily newspapers," *Political Communication and Persuasion* 4: 1–9.

Pierre, R. (2001) "Hate groups use attack to recruit members" *Washington Post* November 10: A6.

"Pig brutality" (1970) *The Black Panther* February 21: 2–27.

Pincus, W. (2001) "House hikes espionage funds" *Washington Post* October 6: A3.

Porzecanski, A. (1973) *Uruguay's Tupamaros*, New York: Praeger.

Potok, M. (2000) "The year in Hate" *National Forum* spring: 32–6.

Powers, T. (1973) *The War at Home: Vietnam and the American people*, New York: Grossman.

Raspberry, W. (2001) "Terrorism's fertile fields" *Washington Post* October 1: A21.

"Religious split among blacks" (1973) *US News & World Report* February 5.

Rich, F. (2001a) "The day before yesterday" *New York Times* September 15: A23.

Rich, F. (2001b) "The end of the beginning" *New York Times* September 29: A23.

Rieff, D. (1993) *The Exile: Cuba in the heart of Miami*, New York: Simon & Schuster.

Risen, J. and Thomas, J. (1998) *Wrath of Angels*, New York: Basic Books.

Rosenthal, R. (2000) *Rookie Cop: Deep undercover in the Jewish Defense League*, St Paul MN: Leapfrog Press.

Ross, J. (1993) "Research on contemporary oppositional terrorism in the United States" in K. Tunnell (ed.) *Political Crime in Contemporary America*, New York: Garland Publishing.

Ross, J. and Gurr, T. (1989) "Why terrorism subsides: a comparative study of Canada and the United States" *Comparative Politics* 21 July: 405–26.

Rothman, S. and Lichter, S. (1982) *Roots of Radicalism: Jews, Christians and the New Left*, New York: Oxford University Press.

Rowan, C. (1996) *The Coming Race War in America*, Boston MA: Little Brown.

Rushdie, S. (2001) "Fighting the forces of invisibility" *Washington Post* October 2: A25.

Russ, S. (1981) *Zionist Hooligans: the Jewish Defense League*, New York: City University of New York.

Safire, W. (2001a) "New day of infamy" *New York Times* September 12: A27.

Safire, W. (2001b) "Equal time for Hitler?" *New York Times* September 20: A31.

Sale, K. (1973) *SDS*, New York: Random House.

Sanchez, R. (2001) "Anti-abortion Web site handed a win" *Washington Post* March 29: A1.

Sanger, D. and Kahn, J. (2001) "Bush freezes assets linked to terror net" *New York Times* September 25.

Sarratt, R. (1966) *The Ordeal of Desegregation*, New York: Harper & Row.

Sater, R. (1996) "Bombings involving Jewish extremists in the United States" *TVI Report* 11: 9–12.

Sater, W. (1981) *Puerto Rican Terrorists: A possible threat to US energy installations*, Santa Monica CA: Rand.

Scanlans (1971) special issue on guerrilla attacks 1968–70, January.

Schell, J. (1976) *The Time of Illusion*, New York: Vintage.

Schemo, D. and Pear, R. (2001) "Loopholes in immigration policy worked in hijack suspects' favor" *New York Times* September 28: A1.

Schmemann S. (2001) "What would 'victory' mean?" *New York Times* September 16: 1.

Schmid, A. and de Graf, J. (1982) *Violence as Communication*, Beverly Hills CA: Sage.

Schuster, M. (2001) "A national survey of stress reactions after the September 11, 2001, terrorist attacks" *New England Journal of Medicine* November 15: 1507–12.

Scott, J. and Schuman, H. (1988) "Attitude strength and social action in the abortion dispute" *American Sociological Review* 53: 785–93.

Shaved for Battle: Skinheads target America's youth (1987) New York: Anti-defamation League of B'Nai B'rith.

Sheridan, M. (2001) "Tougher enforcement by INS urged" *Washington Post* September 18.

Sherry, S. (1999) "I hate what they say" *Washington Post* February 14: B1.

Shipp, E. (2000) "The Shifflett case" *Washington Post* July 16: B6.

Singular, S. (1987) *Talked to Death: The life and murder of Alan Berg*, New York: Beech Tree Books.

Slevin, P. (2001a) "In anthrax probe, questions of skill, motive" *Washington Post* November 5: A5.

Slevin, P. (2001b) "FBI courting Arab Muslim communities" *Washington Post* September 19: A14.

Small, M. (1988) *Johnson, Nixon, and the Doves*, New Brunswick NJ: Rutgers University Press.

Smith, B. (1994) *Terrorism in America*, Albany NY: State University of New York.

Southern Poverty Law Center (1997) *Ku Klux Klan: A history of racism and violence*, Montgomery AL: SPLC.

Stanton, B. (1991) *Klanwatch: Bringing the Ku Klux Klan to justice*, New York: Weidenfeld.

Stark, R. (1996) *The Rise of Christianity: A sociologist reconsiders history*, Princeton NJ: Princeton University Press.

Steel, R. (2001) "The weak at war with the strong" *New York Times* September 14: A27.

Steiner, G. (1983) *The Abortion Dispute and the American System*, Washington DC: Brookings Institution.

Stern, J. (2000) *The Ultimate Terrorists*, Cambridge MA: Harvard University Press.

Stickney, B. (1996) *All-American Monster: The unauthorized biography of Timothy McVeigh*, Amherst NY: Prometheus Books.

Suro, R. (1998) "Terrorism's new profile: the lone wolf" *Washington Post* July 2: A1, A182.

Swartz, M. (1997) "Family secret" *New Yorker* 73 November 17.

"Terrorism and the left" (1974) *Ramparts* May: 21–7.

"The hunt begins" (1993) *Newsweek* March 8: 22.

Thomas, C. (2001) "Act of war shows terrorists must go" *Baltimore Sun* September 12: 23A.

Tolson, J. (2001) "Fight to the finish: Has a 'clash of civilizations' threatened 'the end of history'?" *US News & World Report* October 1: 36.

Treastor, J. (2001) "For insurers, some failures and rate jumps" *New York Times* September 15.

Tucker, N. and Dvorak, P. (2001) "Lapses plague security at federal buildings" *Washington Post* September 28: A1, 12.

"Undercover policeman" (1965) *New York Times* February 17, 1965: A1.

Uriarte-Gaston, M. (1984) *Cubans in the United States*, Boston MA: Center for the Study of the Cuban Community.

"US Muslims scrutinized in terror probes" (1998) *Washington Post* October 31: A1, 8.

Vander Zanden, J. (1960) "The Klan revival" *American Journal of Sociology* 65: 456–62.

Vasconez, C. (1999) "Neal Bradley's long rampage recalled" *Dayton Daily News* July 19.

Verhovek, S. (2001) "Once appalled by race profiling, many find themselves doing it" *New York Times* September 23: A1.

Volkman, E. (1980) "Othello" *Penthouse* April: 68–74, 156–62.

Wade, W. (1987) *The Fiery Cross: The Ku Klux Klan in America*, New York: Simon & Schuster.

Walsh, M. (2001) "At 8:48 a.m. two 'normal guys' met a moment of transformation" *New York Times* September 16: A1.

Weiner, T. (1992) "Death squad alleged in Puerto Rico" *Philadelphia Inquirer* January 26: 4.

Weinraub, B. (2001) "Scratching violence for family fare and patriotism" *New York Times* September 16.

White, J. (1991) *Terrorism: An introduction*, Pacific Grove CA: Brooks-Cole.

Wilgoren, J. (2001) "A terrorist profile emerges that confounds the experts" *New York Times* September 15.

Will, G. (2001) "A strike at the pillars" *Washington Post* September 14: A37.

Wolk, A. (1971) *The Presidency and Black Civil Rights*, Rutherford NJ: Fairleigh Dickinson University Press.

Zaroulis, N. and Sullivan, G. (1984) *Who Spoke Up? American protest against the war in Vietnam*, Garden City NY: Doubleday.

Ziegler, M. (1971) "The Jewish Defense League and its invisible constituency" *New York Magazine* April 19: 28–36.

Zimroth, P. (1974) *Perversions of Justice: The prosecution and acquittal of the Panther 21*, New York: Viking.

Index

154   *Index*